The Green Iguana Manual

FROM THE EXPERTS AT
ADVANCED VIVARIUM SYSTEMS℠

By Philippe de Vosjoli
with Susan Donoghue, V.M.D., D.A.C.V.N.,
Roger Klingenberg, D.V.M., and David Blair

THE HERPETOCULTURAL LIBRARY®
Advanced Vivarium Systems®
Mission Viejo, California

Preface

This book is an expanded and revised edition of *The General Care and Maintenance of Green Iguanas*, initially published in 1990. Some of the information presented here is significantly different than that provided in the first version. Herpetoculture is a rapidly changing field and all of us, the author included, learn as research and personal experience yield updated information. Hundreds of hours of writing, research, and interviews went into this book. Friends and fellow herpetoculturists also contributed invaluable material and many outstanding photographs. Hopefully, this manual will enrich the lives of our green companions as much as they have enriched our own.

Kristin Mehus-Roe, *editor, project manager*
Nick Clemente, *special consultant*
Jarad Krywicki, *contributing editor*
Designed by Michael Vincent Capozzi
All photos by Philippe de Vosjoli except where otherwise indicated
Rachel Rice, *indexer*

LCCN: 96-183295
ISBN: 1-882770-67-6

Cover photography by David Northcott

An Imprint of BowTie Press®
P.O. Box 6050
Mission Viejo, CA 92690
www.avsbooks.com
1-866-888-5526

We want to hear from you. What books would you like to see in the future? Please feel free to write us with any comments on our AVS books.

Printed in Singapore
10 9 8 7 6 5 4 3 2

The photographs in this book are courtesy of: Chris Estep, pp. 6, 14, 23, 68; David Travis, pp. 7, 9, 17, 25, 46, 47; David Blair, pp. 11, 19, 48, 90, 92, 94; John Tashjian, pp. 12, 88 bottom, 89 top courtesy of San Diego Zoo; Glen Carlzen, pp. 16, 81, 88 top; Roger Klingenberg, pp. 71, 75, 78, 79, 82; Jim Dougherty, pp. 89 bottom. Photo by Chris Estep and Wendell Leopard, pp. 50. Photo by Chris Estep, courtesy of Jeff Jenkins, Avian and Exotic Animal Hospital of San Diego, pp. 77. The illustrations in this book are courtesy of: Kevin Anderson, pp. 31, 34, 36, 37.

CONTENTS

INTRODUCTION

Green iguanas are among the most popular reptile pets. Hailing from tropical America, their dinosaur like appearance, large size, ease of maintenance, and pleasant disposition have justifiably contributed to their popularity.

Over the last two decades, across a significant portion of their range, populations of wild green iguanas have declined because of habitat destruction. In their native countries they have also been hunted for food and leather. Most of the green iguanas supplied to the pet trade are now produced on ranches or farms in Colombia, El Salvador, and other Latin American countries, and offered primarily as juveniles. These farmed iguanas are generally healthier than the wild-caught animals imported in the past. Because of their young age they are very adaptable to captive conditions. As a result of improved quality of imports and the reptile-care information currently available to the public, many juvenile iguanas now reach adulthood in captivity in the United States (probably a higher percentage than in the wild). One consequence of this success at captive rearing is "the green iguana problem." When faced with the requirements of their grown-up green iguanas, increasing numbers of owners are choosing to get rid of them, following a trend that is widespread with dogs and cats. Thousands of green iguanas are abandoned by their owners every year, and increasing numbers of large green iguanas in various states of health are brought to animal shelters and rescue organizations. This trend hurts the reputation of reptile hobbyists.

Animal control issues and health issues related to irresponsible pet care provide fuel for organizations that are against keeping reptiles as pets. As reptile owners, it is critical that we act responsibly and consider the long-term consequences of our choices and actions. Remember, before buying that little green iguana whose entire body fits in your hand, it will eventually grow as large as a medium-sized dog with a comparable body length and potentially longer life span. An adult green iguana requires a closet- or room-sized enclosure. If space is a limiting factor, there are many other reptiles available in the pet trade that remain at a more manageable size.

That said, in the right home and under the proper conditions, a green iguana is one of the finest reptile pets available in terms of both their appearance and their level of responsiveness.

This book was written with the goal of providing new and prospective owners with the most updated information on responsible green iguana care. It also aims to help pet owners establish a positive rapport with these wonderful animals.

CHAPTER 1

MEET THE GREEN IGUANA

General Information

Green iguanas are large, semi-arboreal to arboreal (tree dwelling) lizards of the primarily New World (Americas) family Iguanidae. Green iguanas have comparatively long tails (up to three times the body length), a feature of many arboreal lizards, and a permanent dewlap (gular crest located beneath the throat). The species *iguana* has one or more enlarged scales beneath the tympanum (ear drum) and enlarged nuchal (neck) and dorsal (back) crests. Both males and females have a single row of femoral pores on the underside of the thighs.

The name "iguana" is a Spanish version of the Carib word *iwana*. There are two species of green iguanas, *Iguana iguana*, the green iguana of the pet trade, and *Iguana delicatissima* (the West Indian iguana) from the Lesser Antilles, which is characterized by the lack of an enlarged scale beneath the tympanum. At one time, *Iguana iguana* was divided into two subspecies, *iguana* and *rhinolopha*. The

This female green iguana is unusually attractive.

rhinolopha subspecies was considered to be primarily Central American and characterized by the enlargement and alignment of median scales above the snout. However, the *rhinolopha* subspecies is not presently recognized as valid because there are inconsistencies of these characteristics within given populations and geographical areas. Nonetheless, many of the iguanas from Honduras, as well as the occasional Mexican iguanas that manage to enter the market, develop the tiny horn-like projection(s) once attributed to the *rhinolopha* subspecies.

All *Iguana* species are classified as C.I.T.E.S. (Convention on International Trade in Endangered Species) Appendix II animals, which categorizes them as threatened and requires export permits for transport between countries. C.I.T.E.S. is a multinational agreement, wherein participating nations agree to cooperate in the worldwide conservation of rare and vulnerable plant and animal species. Species listed under Appendix I by C.I.T.E.S. are considered threatened with extinction. International trade of these species is not allowed, although exceptions are made for animals proven to be captive produced. Appendix II listed animals are species that are not currently threatened with extinction but which may become so if international trade is not regulated.

Appendix I lists three iguanas: rock iguanas (*Cyclura* sp.), Fiji Island iguanas (*Brachylophus* sp.), and San Esteban Island chuckwallas, *(Sauromalus varius)*. Under Appendix II, there are an additional three: Galapagos marine iguanas *(Amblyrhynchus cristatus)*, Galapagos land iguanas *(Conolophus* sp.), and green iguanas (*Iguana* sp.).

Distribution

The green iguana occurs from Mexico to southern Brazil, Paraguay, and in the Lesser Antilles. It has been introduced in several areas, including Hawaii and south Florida. *Iguana delicatissima* occurs in the Lesser Antilles, where it is becoming threatened in many areas as a result of exploitation, habitat destruction, and displacement by introduced green iguana populations.

Size

There is considerable variation in the potential adult size of green iguanas, depending on country of origin and the conditions under which they are maintained. As a rule, adult iguanas achieve a length of 4 to 5 feet with occasional specimens reaching a length of 6 feet. Males of some South

American populations can reach a length of nearly 7 feet and weigh up to 18 pounds.

Secondary Sexual Characteristics

Several books claim that green iguanas are sexually dimorphic and can be distinguished visually, but the truth is that differences between the sexes are often subtle and only become obvious in older, sexually mature animals. Some of the broad criteria for distinguishing between sexes include: males grow larger than females; males are not as heavy bodied as females; males develop larger nuchal and dorsal crests than females; males have larger scales beneath the tympanum than females; and, one of the most evident characteristics of older animals, males develop larger, broader jowls than females. Nearly all of these characteristics become more obvious as an animal matures, but they are by no means reliable when dealing with young adult animals. Females from some populations develop dorsal crests as large as males of other populations, or have enlarged scales beneath the tympanum as large as those of males.

There are two secondary sexual characteristics that are consistently reliable as animals mature. In animals at least two years old, males' femoral pores, openings in specialized scales that form secretions that may serve the purpose of scent-marking the environment, are significantly enlarged

This male captive-raised Peruvian iguana is eight months old.

compared to the females' and produce femoral pore secretions that resemble enlarged scales. Females have reduced pores. Older males also develop broad, enlarged jowls; their presence removes any doubt as to the iguana's sex.

In addition to the physical differences, behaviors offer some of the best clues for distinguishing between the sexes. As males become sexually mature they perform frequent head jerking displays (a series of rigid up and down bobs of the head), often followed by a series of short up-down bobs while the head moves from side to side. These displays are eventually performed regularly whenever any iguanas are introduced into the enclosure. Males will also attempt to mount females.

Females rarely demonstrate rigid head jerks, although they often display the series of lateral head bobs. Ultimately, males will mate with females and healthy captive-raised females will lay eggs. These final behaviors will clear up any doubt as to the sex of your iguanas.

Once they are about 2.5 feet long, male iguanas can be sexed by manually everting the hemipenes.

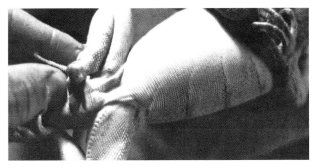

Growth

Within three years a baby iguana grows from a half-ounce hatchling to a 2.5-pound adult—a hundredfold increase in weight. In time, large adults can reach a weight of 10 to 15 pounds, and some South American male iguanas are said to reach 18 pounds. To achieve this degree of growth requires large amounts of food, effective digestion, and enough calcium to build skeletal tissue.

Hatchling iguanas have total lengths (body plus tail) of 7 to 10 inches. By six and a half months, a hatchling iguana fed on a high-quality diet doubles its length, and by about the fifteenth month it triples its original length, reaching a total length of 2 feet to 2.5 feet.

The snout-to-vent length (length of head plus body) of hatchlings ranges from 2.8 to 3.5 inches. In one year it can increase to 8.8 inches and by three years the snout-to-vent length of the mature adults usually exceeds 13.2 inches. The total length of iguanas equals roughly three to three and a half times the snout-to-vent length. Thus, three-year-old iguanas are usually between 3 and 3.5 feet long.

This rapid growth rate means you need to provide an adequate diet that contains enough calcium for the rapidly growing skeleton. It also means providing adequate temperature for effective digestion and, ultimately, a vivarium large enough to accommodate a large reptile. It will quickly become obvious why a minimum 36-inch-long vivarium is recommended for a hatchling iguana.

Green iguanas as large as this 6-foot male are quite rare in captivity.

Green iguanas can reach sexual maturity by two years of age, although the first breeding in captivity often doesn't occur until the third year.

Longevity

With proper care, a green iguana can live ten to fifteen years. Males may live in excess of twenty years. There is one record of a male living almost twenty years and several claims of males reaching twenty-two to twenty-five years.

Varieties and Morphs

The green iguana has a very broad distribution, extending from North America to South America. Depending on a variety of economic, political, and legislative factors, several varieties of iguanas become available to U.S. hobbyists over the course of a year. Depending on the country of origin or locality (particularly insular varieties or island populations), green iguanas vary significantly in color, pattern, length-to-height ratio of the head, crest size, and adult length. These variations are of considerable interest to serious hobbyists and efforts should be made to maintain and captive-breed pure gene pools with these geographical variants. Several of the known variants are presented in this book.

In addition, there are occasional morphs or mutations that hatch in iguana farms or are collected. Unfortunately, many of these odd-colored or patterned iguanas have genetic problems that prevent them from surviving or growing into normal-sized adults. Unusual blue iguanas are occasionally seen among hatchling imports, as are iguanas with increased orange, red, or rose pink coloration. There are also several albino green iguanas in the United States. Captive-bred albinos will probably be available in the future.

This young green iguana is from Aruba Island.

Before You Buy a Green Iguana

There are other factors that limit the pet potential of green iguanas. Once sexually mature, some males become aggressive, particularly during the breeding season.

Owners need to recognize changes in behavior and take precautions to prevent accidents. In addition, a significant percentage of green iguanas harbor *Salmonella* and can present a health risk to owners and family members if proper hygiene procedures are not followed. If you have the time and space (in cold areas, a minimum 6-foot by 4-foot area is required indoors) and if you can enforce strict hygiene procedures among family members, few large reptiles can match the appeal, dragonlike appearance, and personality of a green iguana. To help you make a decision, talk to other green iguana owners and visit with an adult green iguana at a pet store or animal shelter.

This young green iguana was imported from Suriname.

CHAPTER 2

SELECTING YOUR IGUANA

This may be the single most important factor in successfully raising and maintaining an iguana. The selection of a healthy, adaptable animal determines the course of your future owner/pet relationship. When available, select an established, captive-raised animal that is healthy in appearance, active, alert, and extroverted. Size is irrelevant here; it is behavior and apparent health that you should look for. Calm, docile animals that tolerate handling are best.

Unfortunately, it is not always possible to find a healthy captive-raised animal. As a second choice, select a young imported animal.

• Do not purchase imported iguanas over 2 feet long,

especially large adults. Although these animals appear healthy, they are often stressed by captive conditions and will refuse to eat, gradually declining from a parasitic imbalance or disease. Believe it or not, psychological stress can depress the iguana's immune system. In captive breeding projects in Central America, adult animals maintained in large outdoor enclosures generally fail to establish and are eventually released. Most captive propagation programs are based on captive-raised animals.

• Avoid hyperactive iguanas that dash into corners and run madly back and forth when you approach a group of animals. These animals may appear to be active and vigorous, but in reality iguanas that dash into the sides or hide in shelters are wary and easy to panic. This type of iguana usually never makes a good pet, remaining cautious with a low threshold for flight. A scared animal is not the best choice for developing a pet/owner relationship.

• The iguana should be alert, active, and extroverted (remain relatively calm when a hand is placed in their enclosure). Note: In large groups it is normal for iguanas to demonstrate flight behaviors; the flighty ones elicit a flight reaction in other iguanas. Most scatter for a short distance and remain fairly still, while others persist in demonstrating flight behaviors. Avoid the persistently panicked animals because they do not usually become good pets.

Choosing a Healthy Iguana

When selecting a reptile, put aside any notion of saving an ill-looking animal. Sick lizards almost always die—by the time you notice the illness the disease has usually progressed to the point where it is not curable. If you visit a pet store or private owner where the iguanas seem ill or neglected, contact animal control but don't waste your money and set yourself up for disappointment by buying one. Start off right with a healthy lizard.

• Avoid animals that appear thin, listless, or unhealthy, or

This imported adult iguana is close to death. Many imported subadult and adult iguanas do not adjust to captive conditions.

refuse to eat. Low body weight, a dehydrated appearance (loose skin), and a lack of alertness are all danger signs.

• Avoid animals with unusual lumps anywhere on the body, including beneath the skin and along the jaw line.

• Avoid animals with swollen toes, limbs, or lower jaws.

• Avoid animals with eye problems or sunken eyes. The eyes should be round and clear.

• The bellies and tails of the iguanas should be rounded and their bodies not excessively scratched. Avoid animals with asymmetrically distributed areas of darkened skin or black pigmentation.

• The vent area should be clean and free of wet stool or any kind of caking, as should the belly.

• Young iguanas should occasionally flick their tongues as they move about.

Male vs. Female

There are pros and cons to either sex of green iguana. To a significant degree, this choice depends on the expectations of the prospective owner. There are characteristics and problems you may encounter with each respective sex.

Males

Males grow larger than females and develop larger dorsal and nuchal crests. They also develop larger jowls. Males from some areas are significantly more colorful than females, often with extensive amounts of orange, particularly during the breeding season. Some males become aggressive during the breeding season, but their personalities are quite variable. Many males remain tame and docile. A very few male iguanas become aggressive toward female owners during menstruation; however, there is only a very small number of these cases on record to date.

Health Problems: Care must be taken to avoid administering excess calcium and vitamin D_3, particularly in mature males. There appears to be a higher probability of calcium mineralization (metastatic calcification) of internal organs in males than in females.

An adult female green iguana clearly shows the small horns on the snout that are characteristic of green iguanas from Guatemala.

Females

Females do not usually grow as large as males, and they do not usually develop the large dorsal or nuchal crests and large jowls that males do. They are also not as colorful as males. In temperament, female green iguanas vary as much as males, but do not display the unusually aggressive behavior of certain males during the breeding season.

Health Problems: If well cared for, female iguanas will eventually ovulate and lay eggs, but this requires certain dietary and environmental adjustments. Unfortunately, some female iguanas become egg-bound and require veterinary treatment. The failure to provide a suitable egg-laying site may be a primary cause of egg retention in captive female iguanas. Other factors include diet, the health of the animal, disease, the type of heat provided, and other environmental factors. I suspect that females with infertile eggs are more likely to become egg-bound than females with fertile eggs. During the breeding season, provide extra calcium and D_3 in the diet of female iguanas.

This is a private breeding facility for the captive propagation of *Cyclura* species and other iguanas.

CHAPTER 3

QUARANTINE AND ACCLIMATION

W hen first obtained, properly house your new iguana and allow it a period of two to four weeks to adapt to its new home and surroundings. Most newly imported iguanas go through an initial adjustment period, during which they are stressed and may hide and refuse food. Larger specimens imported from the wild may puff up and whip their tails whenever you near their enclosure.

In recently imported iguanas, a normal reaction to the presence of large, moving objects is a flight or fight reaction. This is a stress reaction involving the sympathetic nervous system that can, if it persists over time, inhibit appetite and depress the immune system. For this reason, allow your iguana time to settle in without handling or bothering it. Instead, establish a maintenance schedule and activity routine, offering food and water (or an electrolyte solution) once a day. During this acclimation period, keep your distance from the front of the iguana enclosure, particularly if your iguana is showing signs of stress.

Within two to four weeks, it will be obvious if your iguana is adjusting well. Acclimated animals feed regularly and begin to gain rather than lose weight. Weight loss is usually noticed at the base of the tail, which loses its roundness. Weight gain is seen in a rounding out of the tail from the tail tip to the tail base. Later, the hip area rounds out. Acclimated animals have rounded tails, are alert, feed daily, and show signs of growth. Once acclimated you can work with your iguana to develop a good pet/owner relationship.

In any large group of iguanas, a number will not acclimate to captivity, rapidly losing weight and eventually dying. If caught early enough, some of these animals may turn around with oral administration of electrolytes, glucose, and a high-energy food supplement. With veterinary assistance, their chances of survival are also somewhat increased. The big question is, at what cost? Will a very stressed animal be stressed in the future? The conditions of captivity exert their own pressures and a small percentage of animals will not survive. With proper care, however, a considerably large percentage of captive-raised iguanas survive and live long and happy lives.

Establishing Young Iguanas

1) Pick out an apparently healthy iguana using the selection guidelines in this book.

2) Set up your iguana properly, following the instructions in this book. Provide a heat source and initially set the iguana up on newspaper to observe stool samples. Healthy iguana stools are semi-soft with some definite form. Runny, watery, or bloody stools are signs of possible health problems.

3) Provide a shallow container with clean water.

4) Mist your iguanas once or twice daily before 4 PM. Misting during the day allows the iguanas and their enclo-

sures enough exposure to heat to dry before nightfall.

5) Once or twice daily offer finely shredded, high-calcium vegetables, mixed vegetables, and fruits with a vitamin/mineral supplement. A good alternative is to offer a commercial iguana diet. If the animal does not start feeding within a week, consult a veterinarian to initiate forced feeding.

6) Have a qualified reptile veterinarian perform a fecal check and treat the iguana accordingly. Many people have raised outstanding iguanas without an initial veterinary consultation; however, there are many opportunities for infection in the course of the various trade transactions along an iguana's route to its final home.

7) Do not handle your pet for the first few weeks after bringing it home. Ideally, do not handle hatchling iguanas until they are at least three months old. If the hatchlings are skittish and running into the sides of the tank, provide a shelter and cover half of the front of the enclosure.

8) Handle young iguanas with care. Often, eager new owners and their children handle newly purchased iguanas too frequently and inappropriately. Grabbing baby iguanas by the tail can result in them dropping their tails and grabbing the limbs of young iguanas can lead to disarticulation or fracture of a limb.

Acclimating Adult Imported Iguanas

Relatively few wild-caught adult iguanas are imported into the pet trade, but these occasionally become available to herpetoculturists, either as legal imports or as animals confiscated by customs or wildlife agents. The following steps are recommended for acclimating these iguanas.

1) Have the animal examined by a qualified veterinarian, and checked and treated for internal parasites.

2) Set up the iguana in a large enclosure with appropriate heat, light, basking branch, and a large, shallow container with water.

3) Cover at least two-thirds of the front of the enclosure to minimize any sources of stress.

4) Offer a variety of foods daily, including some bright-

colored fruits and vegetables, such as carrots, strawberries, sweet potatoes, tomatoes, and pitted plums. Don't just offer the food in a dish but also scatter some on the floor of the enclosure.

5) Monitor the animal closely. If it originally had good weight, allow it two weeks to start feeding. One technique that can get wild-caught adults to feed is introducing established immature animals into the cage. The feeding activity of other iguanas often incites a wild-caught animal to start feeding (however, this procedure entails the risk of infecting the established animals with a disease that is infecting the adult). Do not introduce an established adult male with a wild-caught one; you could end up with a bloody mess.

If the iguana has not eaten after about two weeks, consider trying to force-feed a blended diet if it is losing too much weight. Force-feeding requires two people: one to hold the animal and the other to introduce food into the mouth. It is difficult to open the mouth of an adult iguana if it is unwilling to do so. Consult a qualified veterinarian during this process. He or she will have procedures that can significantly increase the chances of acclimating wild-caught iguanas to captivity. With patience and perseverance, some wild-caught adult iguanas will start feeding. Once that happens, the animal will be on its way to becoming established.

Establishing Green Iguanas in Pet Stores

1) Initially select healthy green iguanas. Avoid thin, listless, puffy-eyed, or gaping animals. Avoid animals with damaged skin, soft stools, or caked stool around the vent area.

2) Following purchase, thoroughly wash each individual animal with lukewarm water to remove any dirt, grime, or stool residues adhering to the body. Do not allow the animal to soak in a pan of water or drink any of the water during this process. Because baby iguanas are often kept in crowded conditions at the facilities of both exporters and importers, there is a high probability that disease-causing bacteria and parasites are present on the skin surface.

This iguana pen is in a reptile store. A tame adult iguana on display can significantly increase iguana sales in pet stores.

Examine each animal individually. Separate questionable animals from healthy ones.

3) Set up the animals on a newspaper substrate, with an overhead heat source (use an incandescent bulb in a reflector) and a shallow water dish of clean water or Gatorade (only offer Gatorade for the first week). Lightly mist the animals once or twice daily. If the store temperature is cold, particularly at night, provide an additional secondary heat source, such as a reptile heating pad. Use the additional heater on one side of the enclosure only, so the animals can get away from the heat source.

4) Take stool samples (easy to obtain on newspaper) and a few representative animals to your veterinarian for an examination and fecal check to determine the presence of internal parasites and the best protocol for treatment. After this step, you can set up green iguanas on alfalfa pellets.

5) Feed finely shredded food and/or a commercial iguana diet daily, as indicated under **Diet and Feeding Management**. Remove the food after two hours and offer additional food a second time in the course of the day. This procedure can result in more frequent feeding by iguanas. Thin animals or animals that do not feed after a few days should be fed soft baby foods administered through a large syringe. Consult your veterinarian to guide you in this.

6) Monitor animals carefully. Always isolate ill-appearing animals from healthy ones. Seek veterinary assistance if anything looks awry.

7) It is reasonable to charge extra for healthy, parasite-treated, and veterinarian-examined green iguanas.

This male Peruvian green iguana exhibits extensive bluish green and light blue coloration common in iguanas from Peru.

CHAPTER 4

IGUANAS AS PETS

The key to developing a good relationship with your iguana is for you to become completely non-threatening to it. It is easiest to develop this type of relationship with younger animals or captive-raised adults that are already kept as pets. With frequent interaction, a pet iguana essentially becomes so accustomed to humans that they fail to elicit any type of flight or fight reaction. The result is a pet that remains calm when approached, allows itself to be petted, picked up, and carried, comes toward its owner when approached with a dish of food, feeds from its owner's hand, and remains relatively calm when moved within the home. When iguanas lose their fear of humans, they are one of the best and most rewarding reptile pets.

Once your new iguana is acclimated, begin short daily sessions of interaction. Remember, iguanas are not birds or dogs or cats; they don't like to be fondled or petted for extended periods of time. They shouldn't be taken out in public; not only because they may become frightened and you risk losing them, but also because the public display of reptiles outside of a proper context (usually an educational forum such as a herp show or a school display) often frightens people and perpetuates the notion that herpetoculturists are irresponsible.

People have different approaches to working with iguanas. Some begin by working with an iguana within its cage, scratching the back of the neck or gently stroking the sides, then slowly picking it up and placing it back in its cage. Others prefer taking the animal out of the cage and having brief taming sessions, where the animal is calmly coaxed to move from hand to hand. Initially, iguanas will try to dash away, but if caught and encouraged over several attempts to move slowly from hand to hand or from hand to arm, they usually calm down. This is the first step to accustoming your iguana to being picked up. Handling sessions should be brief, no more than fifteen minutes at a time, up to two or three times a day. After several days or weeks you will notice that your iguana remains calmer. Let its behavior dictate the extent to which it is left out of its cage in a given iguana area.

How tame an iguana becomes depends on how much time and effort an owner invests into interacting with the animal. Some iguanas become so tame that they will remain on a platform at a herp fair, allowing themselves to be observed and petted by dozens of adults and children. At these shows there are also people with tame iguanas on their shoulders. There is even a man in Los Angeles, California, who owns a large group of iguanas that are so docile he can pose them in costumes for photographs.

Stress and the Iguana

Subadult and adult green iguanas are creatures of familiarity. They are often stressed when placed in situations that expose them to unfamiliar stimuli. For example, if you move an iguana into a new cage in a different room of the house, it may go off feed for a week and even bash its head into the sides of the new cage by running around in a panic. If a group of iguanas is used to only having certain people take care of them, they may panic and run into the sides of their cage when someone unfamiliar or wearing unusually bright-colored clothes walks by their cage. Selling or buying an older iguana, with the subsequent transfer to a new location, frequently results in a period of stress/adjustment during which an animal refuses to feed.

You can prevent stress reactions through frequent and regular interaction with a variety of people. Allowing iguanas to establish themselves in a new environment by partially covering an enclosure, providing a shelter, and minimizing exposure to unfamiliar humans for a few weeks also reduces stress reactions.

Broken-hearted Iguana

One sad case of stress in an iguana involved a beautiful captive-raised animal that had been kept impeccably and was cherished by a young girl. Because of custody issues between her divorced parents, she had to sell her iguana to a local pet store. She entered the pet store with her grandfather, the iguana on her shoulder, and cried as she relinquished her pet and companion. The iguana was placed in a large glass display case exposed to the general public. It didn't feed and barely moved after it was placed in the cage. After three days separated from its owner and stressed by the unfamiliar conditions of the store, the animal died. The question remains: can an iguana die of a broken heart?

Zoning Out

Adult green iguanas, usually older males, sometimes deal with stress through a peculiar behavior that, for want of a better term, I call zoning out. Essentially, the iguana shuts off by closing its eyes and appearing as if it has suddenly fallen asleep. Sometimes an iguana does this when someone pets them; at other times they do this when surrounded by a number of strange people. In ethological terms, this type of behavior appears to be the result of the interaction of drives. At one level, the iguana wants to escape or possibly perform an aggressive display; at another, it wants to remain still. It does the latter but shuts off visual input and enters a trance.

Cage-Free Iguanas

There are iguana owners who allow their pets the run of a room in the house. This is not a good idea unless you can allocate one room and design it in a way that accommodates the pet. In a normal living situation, iguanas can get tangled in electrical cords, topple things, scratch furniture, and ruin curtains. In addition, the Centers for Disease Control cautions against allowing green iguanas free range of a home because they can spread salmonellosis.

Iguanas kept in room-sized enclosures often defecate in a preferred area or corner of the room. Placing a large pan with alfalfa pellets in the preferred corner makes iguana maintenance in such set-ups relatively easy.

Salmonellosis

This is a disease caused by bacteria of the genus *Salmonella*. It can be transmitted from infected animals, such as green iguanas, to humans. In humans, salmonellosis causes nausea, vomiting, and diarrhea; in severe cases it can cause paralysis, coma, and (rarely) death. Young children, immunosuppressed adults, and older people can die if infected with *Salmonella*.

To avoid contracting salmonellosis, always wash your hands after handling green iguanas. Teach children not to kiss iguanas or put their fingers in their mouths when handling iguanas.

Iguana Personalities

Anyone who has worked with iguanas knows that iguanas have different personalities. Some are outgoing and appear to enjoy interactions with humans, while others are nervous, shy, and scared. Some iguanas are easily aggravated and anti-social, readily lashing out with their tails. As a result, not all iguanas make great pets. Some just tolerate humans and are best considered good vivarium display animals. Give care to initially selecting a calm, outgoing animal (the small, healthy-appearing iguana that comes over and grabs a section of lettuce from your hand). If you don't have good luck with one animal as a pet, don't give up; try another. As a general rule, starting off with calm, fearless babies with whom you regularly interact early on will result in a rewarding owner/pet interrelationship.

Iguana Bites

Like dogs, all green iguanas are not created alike. Their personalities vary and can change after sexual maturity sets in. In males, this means a surge in testosterone that leads to territorial and sexual behaviors, as well as aggression. In some cases, tame animals can become actively aggressive, going out of their way to bite someone. An aggressive adult male iguana can be dangerous. A single bite can result in serious injury costing thousands of dollars in medical treatment. With some males, these behaviors are seasonal and can be corrected using properly applied negative reinforcement methods. Positive reinforcement (rewarding when an iguana behaves as desired) will not work in the case of a hormone-crazed male iguana. A male iguana that becomes aggressive is usually territorial and will challenge your status. The only way to get the animal to stop this behavior is to act as an alpha male. That means not backing down if charged and using the soft end of a broom to whack the aggressive iguana (this simulates lashing with the tail) until it runs away from you. As you do this yell "No!" and chase it a short distance if necessary.

Aggressive behavior in males may only be seasonal in some animals, but certain males are difficult to deal with no matter what you do. Some of them may also be very aggressive toward female iguanas in close quarters. However, many male iguanas remain gentle toward their owners, only directing aggressive behaviors toward other male iguanas.

I've heard of a number of green iguana bites that required either stitches or surgery. I had an employee who was bitten down to the bone by a small male rhinoceros iguana entering sexual onset. Whatever you do, remember that iguana bites are serious business. As with dog bites, do not take these attacks lightly. Assert your authority or run the risk of serious injury.

Because of consistent aggression and unpredictability, some iguanas are unsuitable as pets. Although some claim that castration effectively reduces aggression, there are cases where euthanasia is the only recourse. Frightened or threatened iguanas may also bite, particularly when grabbed. Heed the warning signals of frightened animals, such as hissing or tail whipping. When handling a frightened iguana, use a towel to cover the animal and wear heavy-duty gloves.

CHAPTER 5

THE LIFE STAGES OF GREEN IGUANAS

Like most larger forms of life, reptiles undergo ontogeny (different life stages) from egg fertilization to old age. For reptile keepers, a simple model of ontogeny divides development into five life stages.

1) **Prebirth/embryonic.** Besides a brief period inside the mother that follows the initial fertilization of an ovum, this stage is spent enclosed within a shelled egg. The mother's genetics, diet, and health, as well as incubation temperature, substrate composition, moisture, and the risk of predation all directly affect this stage. In green iguanas, incubation temperature can also affect the tail length. This stage lasts eight to twelve weeks, depending on incubation temperature, and ends with the emergence of a hatchling from the egg.

2) **Hatchling/juvenile.** Baby green iguanas, like many reptiles, are initially flight prone because it is their only

Partly because of their size, juvenile and adult iguanas exploit different niches and resources.

form of defense. They show no territorial behaviors and little aggression either toward humans or each other. As they get larger, frightened animals may tail whip, but this usually will not happen with captive-raised green iguanas that receive regular exposure to humans. The small size of baby green iguanas has both advantages and constraints, linked in part to their relative surface-to-volume ratio. A rule of physics is that all other things being equal (such as the general form of a green iguana), a smaller object has a greater relative surface-to-volume ratio than a larger one. In short, a baby green iguana has proportionately much more skin area for its weight and length than an adult. Thus, when basking, baby green iguanas heat up more quickly than large iguanas. They also cool down faster when exposed to cold. It also means that for their size, they're lighter than a large iguana and can run at a surprising speed.

A characteristic of this stage is a noticeably high growth rate. Hatchling iguanas do not stay small for long. This growth rate requires that young iguanas ingest significant amounts of calcium to build their fast-growing skeletons. Not providing adequate amounts of calcium and vitamin D_3 is the main reason metabolic bone disease (MBD) is one of the most frequently encountered diseases at this stage. See **Diseases and Disorders** for more information on this disease.

3) **Sexual onset.** Depending on how they're raised, sexual onset, which is linked to the maturation of sex organs and the production of sex hormones, occurs sometime between two and three years of age, at a length of about 3 feet. In males, the changes in appearance and behavior can be drastic. As with adolescent male humans, male green iguanas bulk up and show a steady growth rate for a couple of years following sexual onset. Male iguanas also develop large jowls, tall dorsal crests, and varying amounts of orange.

Sexual onset males also start displaying territorial and aggressive behaviors that can be directed toward their owners with serious consequences. The main characteristic of this stage is reproduction. Males expend energy to fend off other males and attempt to breed with females. Females ovulate and lay eggs. Toward the end of this stage, at around five years, kidney disease becomes a significant cause of death in green iguanas, usually because of the failure of owners to provide enough heat, water, and humidity. It can take up to 300 watts worth of incandescent spotlights to adequately heat a large iguana. Remember, large iguanas heat and cool more slowly than small ones.

The next stage is distinguished by achieving a near maximum size and a drastic decline in growth rate. In short, the iguana has stopped growing.

4) **Mature adult.** Around six to eight years, growth rate slows down to the point of being nearly insignificant. Activity levels become reduced and tend to occur in spurts. Larger iguanas usually spend long periods of time in one place. In the wild, large, mature iguanas have few enemies and both large males and females are in a size category that limits competition with smaller sexual-onset animals. They're simply in a different league.

Mature iguanas, like humans, are generally more settled. By the time an iguana reaches this stage, it has a low surface-to-volume ratio, requiring extra effort on the part of owners to provide adequate heat. At this stage, a primary cause of death of captive animals is kidney disease.

5) **Old age.** Most animals, either in the wild or in captivity, never see this stage. Nature does not select for longevity but for reproductive success. The signs may be subtle but old green iguanas become less active, feed less, and may show problems shedding. Females usually stop breeding. This stage ends with death.

As iguanas mature, their relationships with other creatures change.

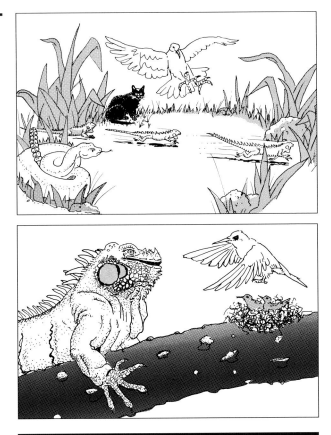

Understanding Surface to Volume Ratios

The general rule is that a small object has a larger surface-to-volume ratio than a larger similar object. In terms of iguanas, a small iguana has a proportionately larger skin area than a large iguana. This means that when exposed to a heat source, small green iguanas can warm up faster than large iguanas.

As an example let us consider two cubes. Cube A has 1-inch sides. Its surface is 1 x 1 x 6 = 6 square inches. Its volume is 1 x 1 x 1 = 1 cubic inch. The surface-to-volume ratio is 6 to 1.

Now, let us consider a larger cube with 2-inch sides. Its surface is 2 x 2 x 6 = 24 square inches and its volume is 2 x 2 x 2 = 8 cubic inches. Its surface-to-volume ratio is 24 to 8, or 3 to 1. Using this example, it is clear that as an object becomes larger its relative surface area becomes smaller. This has implications for all reptile keepers. Baby reptiles heat up and cool faster. For their size, the weight of baby reptiles is proportionately less than that of larger reptiles.

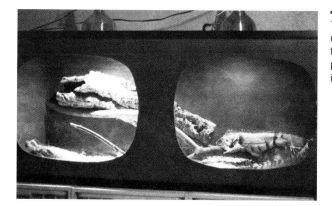

This cage was custom-made for an adult pair of green iguanas.

CHAPTER 6

HOUSING AND GENERAL MAINTENANCE

Enclosure Size

Once they reach 2.5 to 3 feet, keep green iguanas singly (one per enclosure), except for short breeding introductions. In room-sized enclosures, one male can be kept with several females, but the group must be carefully monitored.

Selection of an enclosure is an important consideration for the well being of your iguana. Because initial growth for the first two years is quite rapid, you should not start off with an enclosure that is too small. As a starter tank for a hatchling or juvenile iguana, purchase a standard 29-gallon (30 inches long) or 30-gallon (36 inches long) all-glass tank with screen cover. They are readily available, easy to clean, and provide good visibility. This should accommodate the iguana for the first twelve to eighteen months. Later, you will have to move up to a 55-gallon (48 inches

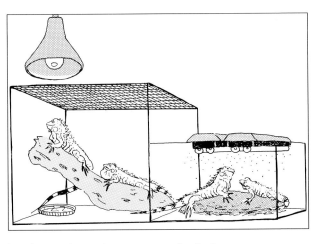

long) aquarium. To save money in the long run, you may find it more economical to purchase a larger enclosure right away.

For animals 4 feet or larger, you will need to purchase a custom-built enclosure. An iguana enclosure should be at least 1.5 times the length of the animal in width and .75 the length of the animal in height. Enclosures can be built of wood with a glass front, screen top, or small, screen side panels. The door(s) can be on the front (framed glass) or sides. Some people successfully use 1-inch square vinyl-coated welded wire on a wood frame to house large iguanas. This type of wire is also used in birdcage construction, but finding a source may require investigation. Another solution for keeping large adult iguanas is to partition a room into a room-size cage. Iguanas can be kept in smaller cages if a large pen is built for daytime activity.

Maintenance

Iguanas are relatively clean animals. They often defecate in a given area, which makes maintenance easy because you simply need to place newspaper or a tray with sand in that area.

The cage substrate for iguanas can be as simple as newspaper or brown paper, which makes cleaning and changing easy, or it can consist of fine- to medium-grade orchid bark, which is attractive but requires periodic changing. Orchid bark has the advantage of being able to absorb moisture, providing air humidity without a wet surface. One substrate that is highly recommended for iguanas is alfalfa pellets (rabbit pellets). They are inexpensive, absorbent, and can safely be ingested. In fact, hungry iguanas will actually eat the pellets.

Dirty Vivarium Glass and Nasal Salt Discharge

Depending on the diet you feed your iguana, you may notice that the glass of your iguana enclosure frequently becomes coated with whitish spots. The cause is usually the nasal discharge of iguanas. Like many other vegetarian lizards, green iguanas have nasal salt glands that essentially allow them to sneeze excess salts. If a diet heavy in salts is offered, iguanas may even accumulate white salt encrustations on the rims of their nostrils.

Landscaping the Vivarium

Both an iguana enclosure and an iguana pen should have branches lying diagonally across the enclosure (the branches should be of a diameter slightly larger than the iguana's body) as basking and resting sites. Arrange the branches so that the iguana can warm itself yet maintain enough of a distance from the spotlight to prevent thermal burns. With newly purchased iguanas, particularly when

Iguanas will utilize basking branches and resting sites.

imported, supply a shelter during the acclimation period. Place a heating pad set on low or medium heat beneath the shelter. Once the iguana is acclimated, remove the shelter to discourage hiding and avoiding interaction.

Iguana Pens

Iguana pens are platforms raised on legs and placed near screened windows or under spotlights that allow larger iguanas an alternative to remaining in a small cage all day. Use these only with larger adult iguanas that are established and not prone to flight behaviors. As a rule, adult iguanas are much less active than juveniles; if the conditions are right, both males and females will spend hours perched on thick wood branches anchored onto the raised platform. Stores often use this method to display tame adults. In homes, do not place adults in pens without supervision to prevent their leaving the area. Provide thick wood perches for resting areas and place under a heat/UV source. Line the edges of the platform with a raised edge to contain the substrate material and present a visual barrier.

CHAPTER 7

HEATING AND HUMIDITY

Temperature

Temperature is a critical factor in the successful rearing and maintenance of green iguanas. The microflora of the hindgut (bacterial and protozoal flora of the enlarged proximal portion of the large intestine) that make iguanas so effective at digesting and extracting nutrients from fiber require relatively high temperatures to perform their task. For effective digestion, iguanas must be able to raise their body temperatures to 88° F. High temperatures are also essential for the immune system to fight off disease.

In the vivarium, provide heat with an incandescent spotlight placed above the screen or outside of the screened area of the enclosure. The heat levels on basking areas closest to the bulb should reach 95-100° F. It is critical that the bulbs are separated from iguanas by a screen partition because iguanas will lie against the bulbs until they are severely burned. Thermal burns caused by inattentive owners are a common veterinary problem with lizards. So, remember, keep your lizard away from the bulb.

The advantage of spotlights over other heat sources is that they allow iguanas to thermoregulate by lateral basking and by varying their distance from the heat. Lateral basking, which consists of the animal presenting its sides to a heat source, is usually practiced by arboreal animals. Many arboreal lizards are laterally flattened so they can present a large surface area to sun rays striking their sides.

Hot rocks should not be used with iguanas because they are essentially all or nothing, usually 95-110° F or no heat. With hot rocks, lizards can only warm up by applying their bellies to the hot surface. That's okay for ground-dwelling lizards, but of questionable value for green iguanas. In the wild, green iguanas bask by directing themselves toward the sun, not by sitting on hot rocks. Aside from the risk of skin damage as a result of long-term direct contact with a high heat source, there is a chance that other veterinary problems, such as damage to internal organs, can develop as a result of this abnormal behavior. Hot-rock type heaters also provide some owners an excuse for not supplying an adequate light source. Many owners mistakenly believe that they do not need to provide light when a hot rock provides heat. Unfortunately, many pet stores promote that thinking by displaying baby green iguanas in dark or poorly lit vivaria, with the only heat provided by misused hot rocks.

During the day, set lights on a timer so that they are on twelve to fourteen hours a day, with a temperature of 85-95° F. At night, adult iguanas can be safely maintained at temperatures as low as 65° F, as long as they are allowed to warm up during the day. Juveniles are best kept at higher temperatures (74-80° F at night). To heat iguana cages at night, use heating pads, heat strips, thermostatically controlled pig blankets (available through feed stores), heat tape, or red incandescent bulbs. Follow directions carefully when using heating pads and heat cables to prevent fire. Separate red light bulbs from the iguanas with screening.

Heat is the Word

Many of the problems encountered with green iguanas can be attributed to poor diet and inadequate heat levels. A common error is using the same size spotlight as an iguana grows up, which will eventually make it difficult for an adult iguana to achieve its optimal operating temperature. With large iguanas, it is best to use two spotlights over a basking area so that heat is distributed over a wider radius than with a single bulb. Feeding green iguanas under low temperatures can lead to gout. Inadequate heat can also make calcium absorption less efficient. Providing the right amount of heat is of critical importance to the welfare of green iguanas in captivity.

Sunlight and Ultraviolet Radiation

Experimental evidence indicates that exposure to ultraviolet-B (UV-B) radiation in the 290 to 305 nanometer range (a nanometer is a measurement of light frequency—one billionth of a meter) allows green iguanas to synthesize vitamin D_3, which is required for calcium absorption and other metabolic functions. Special light meters can be purchased to measure the amount of UV-B produced by a bulb, but they are very expensive. A cheap, low-precision UV-B photosensitive card was recently offered by a bulb manufacturer and may be useful if you want to obtain a rough measurement of output differences between commercial bulbs.

Although many green iguanas are kept successfully for ten years or more without exposure to a UV source, some experts believe that exposure to UV-B is essential for achieving greater longevity. The least expensive way to expose green iguanas to UV-B is to place them in an outdoor cage and allow them to bask in sunlight. The cage must be partially shaded so that they can get away from excessive heat when they desire. For those who do not have the facilities for outdoor caging or who live in cold climates, provide sunlight through an open, screened window or a Mylar window panel. The other widely used and recommended alternative is to supply a UV-generating light source, such as the high-output UV-B fluorescent reptile bulbs currently on the market. Recently, mercury vapor spotlights, which generate a good level of UV radiation and heat, have become available for use with reptiles. There are companies offering self-ballasting (you can screw it into an ordinary bulb socket) mercury vapor UV-B reptile spotlights that produce enough UV-B to substitute for sunlight, allowing green iguanas to synthesize vitamin D_3. Always follow the directions on the label.

Relative Humidity

Relative humidity is important in helping a green iguana maintain a proper hydration level and may help reduce water loss through the skin and during breathing. A relative humidity of at least 60 percent, and preferably 70 to 80 percent, is recommended for green iguanas. In dry areas, cool air humidifiers are useful in helping to raise the relative humidity of a room. There are several temperature and humidity gauges sold in the trade that will allow you to assess the conditions of your enclosures. As you will notice, green iguanas maintained at the right humidity level also have more supple, softer skin. Consider offering a large, shallow dish of water periodically. This can raise the relative air humidity in the vivarium while providing a place for soaking, which facilitates shedding.

Other ways to raise relative air humidity include daily misting or providing a container with a piece of foam rubber three-quarters filled with water. The surface will be slightly moist but no water will be accessible for ingestion. Evaporated water will provide humidity. The foam and the container can be easily watched.

Misting

Lightly mist iguanas once a day several hours before the lights are turned off (so all water droplets can evaporate). This is especially important for juvenile iguanas. The mist provides water and humidity and facilitates shedding.

CHAPTER 8

GROOMING

I guanas cannot be groomed in the proper sense, but attention to appearance is beneficial to their health and facilitates their handling.

Claw Trimming

Most iguana setups do not offer enough rough surface areas or enough space for iguanas to wear down their claws. Furthermore, iguanas naturally develop sharp, pointed claws that can inflict superficial skin damage. If you trim the claw points on a regular basis, you will have an iguana pet that can be picked up without damaging you or your clothes.

Claw trimming requires two people and good lighting. One person holds the iguana with both hands, one hand encircling the neck and the area above the forelegs and the other hand encircling the area above the hindlegs, while the other person trims the claws. The animal should be positioned so that the tail is stabilized against the body or a table surface. Once the animal is held firmly, turn it vertically or sideways so that the ventral area (belly) is facing the person doing the claw trimming. Trim claws as follows:

1) Apply rubbing alcohol or an antiseptic cream to a cotton swab and clean off the claws of foot to be trimmed.

2) Hold one digit at the base of the claw and look carefully under the light. In young iguanas, you will see blood vessels running into the claw that appear as a thin black line. Using dog or cat nail clippers, clip the sharp point in front of the blood vessel. After clipping, use a nail file to file any sharp edges down. Clipping the nails requires attention and meticulous care. In larger iguanas, the claws appear a solid dark color and blood vessels are not always visible. Only clip the pointed end of the claws. Sometimes clipping off the sharp point of a claw will lead you to accidentally clip through the blood vessels. If this happens, wipe the claw involved with a disinfectant then dip the bleeding tip in cornstarch or styptic powder. Remember, only clip off the sharp point of the claw. Clipping the claw base can result in serious bleeding and infection. With some attention, nail clipping is relatively simple once you are experienced with it.

If you are uncomfortable clipping your iguana's nails, visit a bird groomer (it's essentially the same process) or your veterinarian.

Bathing

General cleanliness is essential for the long-term well being of your iguana. Offer your iguana the opportunity to bathe in a large container of lukewarm water every one or two weeks. Leave the water in the enclosure for only a few hours. After your iguana has bathed, remove any pieces of shed skin left attached to body or to the hands, feet, or toes. You can slide shed remains off the dorsal crest scales as long as the shed skin is partially detached from the scales; the premature removal of shed skin is harmful to an iguana. An alternative to bathing is a thorough misting. Do any kind of bathing or misting early in the day so the iguana is dry by nightfall.

Iguana Handling Dos and Don'ts

Do not grab or pick up iguanas by their limbs or tails; this can result in lost tails and broken limbs. Encourage tame iguanas to climb on you or pick them up with an above-body hold. Untamed iguanas require one hand above the neck/shoulder area and one hand at the hip/base of the tail.

CHAPTER 9

BREEDING

t is not within the scope of this book to cover details of the captive breeding of green iguanas, so the following is just basic information on this topic.

In spite of what is stated in a number of pet books, when kept and fed in the right manner, mature sexual pairs breed readily. One problem with keeping pairs together in a vivarium is that sexually mature males have such a high sex drive that they can bite and tear a female to death in their attempts to pass on their genes. Compared to their body size, male green iguanas have some of the biggest testes of any land vertebrate. As a result, they don't always think with their comparatively small brains. If you are seriously interested in breeding iguanas, consider using room-sized enclosures and ratios of several females per male, or keep animals separate except during breeding introductions.

In the wild, iguanas usually breed during the dry season, when food availability is reduced. The hatching of iguanas, on the other hand, often occurs at the onset of the rainy season, when food is more plentiful. In captivity, reduced photoperiod (hours of light) combined with cooler night temperatures and reduced feeding, often lead to breeding in late winter or early spring. Sometimes, a second breeding occurs in the fall.

Nest Box

Female iguanas with eggs (noticeable by the enlarged belly and lumpy sides) typically go off feed for three to five weeks prior to laying. If you notice this, don't panic; it's normal. The female should appear fat with minimal weight

This is a breeding cage for Peruvian green iguanas. The horizontal basking sites are made of PVC pipes with a heat cable on a rheostat running through their center. They are covered with artificial grass carpeting. An artificial nesting site was made with a kitchen trashcan, half-filled with sandy soil.

loss (though hips may become more prominent during this period). Provide gravid females an egg-laying site after the third week of fast. The easiest method is to dump a mixture consisting of 50 percent moistened potting soil and 50 percent sand in one corner of the enclosure. Over this, place an inverted box with an entrance hole. Alternatively, you can fill a large polystyrene box with moist soil, cover it, and carve a hole out of the side.

Another type of nest box can be made of a tall, rectangular, plastic kitchen trash container. When given a choice, green iguanas usually prefer a long container over a square one. To use a kitchen trash container as a nest box, place it on its side and fill it halfway with a mixture of 50 percent potting soil and 50 percent sand. Tape the lid on the container after cutting out a hole in the upper side of the lid. Place the egg-laying box on its side at one end of the enclosure. Gravid iguanas without a suitable egg-laying site often lay individual eggs in a scattered manner over several days. There is also a risk that they could become egg-bound.

Incubator

Following laying (the female's belly will suddenly appear empty and sagging), remove the eggs and place them in an incubator. You can make an incubator using an aquarium and submersible heater. Simply add enough water in the

Captive-bred rhinoceros iguanas hatch from their shells.

aquarium to cover the submersible heater with at least 1 inch of water, then use bricks or other materials to build a platform over the water. On the platform, place a large container, such as a large food-storage container. Add moistened vermiculite to the container using equal parts vermiculite and purified or drinking water by weight. Cover the container with a lid with numerous holes in it and cover the tank.

The temperature inside the box should be maintained at 84-87° F. Use an electronic digital thermometer with an outdoor sensor, sold in some electronic supply stores. Simply place the sensor inside the incubator and the thermometer will give you a continuous, easy-to-monitor reading. To calibrate the heat, keep a thermometer in the box for the first few hours, checking the temperature every one to two hours. Once the temperature has been calibrated and is stable, bury the eggs in the vermiculite so that part of the upper surface is exposed to the air, and place the cover back on the container. The tank should then be covered with a glass plate with a small slit allowing air to get in. Very lightly mist the surface of the eggs two to three times a week. The eggs should hatch in seventy to ninety days. Green iguanas from a common clutch will hatch in a scattered manner over a period of time, which can extend for eight days.

When green iguana eggs fail to hatch, the usual causes are: infertility, improper incubation temperature, inadequate moisture of the incubating medium, low relative humidity in the incubating container, small yolk size and poor nutrient reserve due to the health or condition of the female, and, more rarely, genetic incompatibility or disease.

If followed, the recommendations in this chapter should allow you to successfully incubate green iguana eggs. In the case of hatching failure, examine the factors listed above to help determine the cause.

The bulk of an iguana's diet should be made up of greens, vegetables, and fruit.

CHAPTER 10

DIET AND FEEDING MANAGEMENT

By Susan Donoghue, V.M.D., D.A.C.V.N.

From their teeth to their tails, green iguanas are designed for living in trees, enjoying sunshine and tropical air, and eating leaves, blossoms, and fruit. Your pet may look like a fire-breathing, flesh-eating dragon, but its anatomy, biology, chemistry, and physiology say otherwise. Pet green iguanas can be fed salads of chopped fresh produce from the supermarket, leaves and blossoms growing in the wild, and commercial iguana foods. Dietary supplements can also be fed as snacks and treats. Follow these guidelines for iguana foods, meal planning, and feeding management:

Food Sources

Greens: Readily available salad greens include endive, escarole, romaine lettuces, amaranth, collards, dandelion, kale, mustard, and spinach. Romaine is a favorite of iguanas.

Packages of chopped, mixed greens are sold in groceries; one of the tastiest for iguanas is "spring mix." Greens form the primary component of salads for iguanas because they are delicious and nutritious. When beginning, purchase small amounts of a variety of greens and see which your iguana prefers.

Once home from the supermarket, greens should be washed in a sink full of cold water, dunking the greens in a strainer or colander so that the dirt sinks to the bottom. Discard dead leaves and pat the rest dry with paper towels. Store in a crisper in the fridge.

The Benefits of Romaine Lettuce

I've heard that lettuce is nutritionally empty but you recommend romaine lettuce. Why?

Fruits and vegetables, including greens, contain about 85 to 95 percent water. Because of this high water content, lettuces have received a bad rap that is undeserved and based on lore instead of fact. Once your iguana eats romaine, the water is absorbed into the body and the water goes a long way toward keeping your iguana healthy. The remaining romaine contains 36 percent plant-protein, 36 percent fibers, vitamin C, calcium, and many additional essential nutrients.

Other Vegetables: Green iguanas enjoy most vegetables. Zucchini, shredded carrot, mild peppers, pumpkin, and shredded sweet potato are colorful, tasty additions to greens. Legumes, including beans (butter, green, lima, snap, and soy) and peas (green, snow, and sugar), are good sources of calcium and plant protein.

Sprouts can also be added to iguana salads. Commercially grown sprouts include legumes (alfalfa, mung bean) and grasses (barley, oats, radish). The *Salmonella* bacterium has been found in commercially grown sprouts, so homegrown sprouts may be safer as well as fresher for your pet.

Fruit: Wild green iguanas eat tropical fruits, and your pet will enjoy commercially available fruits from your supermarket. Favorites are banana, mango, and papaya. Others include apple, fig, guava, kiwi fruit, melon, peach, pear, pineapple, plantain, and watermelon. Iguanas also enjoy berries in their salads. Try blackberries, blueberries, boysenberries, mulberries, raspberries, and strawberries.

A diet of salad and a few supplements will provide complete and balanced nutrition for your iguana. An added benefit of salads is the high water content. Water is critical to the health of your pet.

Leaves and Blossoms: You can offer homegrown plants that are well washed and free of herbicides and pesticides. Clover, dandelion, grape leaves (and fruit), hibiscus, kudzu, nasturtium (and non-marinated capers), pothos, and rose are just a few. Do not offer your iguana any plant if you are not sure of its safety.

Do Not Feed

This short list highlights plants to omit from your iguana's diet. This list is not intended to be all-inclusive, so always check with your veterinarian before offering your iguana a new plant.

Dracaena house plants	Easter lily
Wild cherry	Equisetum
Bracken fern	Avocado
Yew	Mountain laurel
Toxic mushrooms	Rhododendron
Azalea	Jack-in-the-pulpit

To Feed or Not to Feed

On the Internet I've seen lists of foods to avoid feeding my iguana, and I'm confused. These lists contain dozens and sometimes hundreds of plants. Can so many plants be so dangerous for my iguana?

Later in this chapter you'll read about secondary plant compounds. All plants contain substances designed to repel herbivores. The long lists are generated when there is no discrimination between substances, amounts fed, scientifically determined toxic doses, the makeup of the plant, the substance, and the individual iguana. Your veterinarian can explain in detail to you how your iguana tolerates many plants containing secondary plant compounds so that you don't have to avoid plants such as amaranth, apple, clover, kale, spinach, and berries.

Pellets: Commercial diets for green iguanas are primarily dry, pelleted foods made up of corn meal, soybean meal, and other ingredients from the livestock feed industry.

Green iguanas can be raised and maintained successfully when part of their diet consists of commercial dry diets formulated for vegetarian reptiles. Pelleted food should not be the only food offered to green iguanas. The advantages and drawbacks of commercial diets are discussed later in this chapter.

The Importance of Dietary Supplements

Fresh diets for green iguanas require nutrient supplementation because few of the foods in their diets are nutritionally complete or balanced. Most vegetarian foods that are purchased in local markets (greens, carrots, and bananas) are deficient in a variety of essential nutrients, such as calcium and certain amino acids, fatty acids, and trace minerals.

The type and amount of supplementation needed by your iguana depends on several factors. Iguanas housed outdoors with access to the ground will obtain vitamin D_3 from basking in the sun and many trace minerals from access to soil, whereas those kept indoors need these essential nutrients provided in their diet.

Many types of supplements are marketed—some are specifically for green iguanas, while others are for reptiles in general, for animals in general, or for humans. Iguanas have been raised successfully on all types of supplements. The key to success isn't the intended species, but the formulation and completeness of the product and its suitability to the diet being fed. Read labels carefully in order to assess supplements.

Supplemental Calcium: Calcium is critical for healthy bone growth in green iguanas. There are high calcium foods but iguanas usually need supplemental calcium, regardless of dietary components. Most supplements emphasizing vitamins and minerals fail to provide enough calcium to meet the needs of iguanas. Thus, two types of supplements are often necessary—one containing vitamins and minerals (including a little calcium), and a second containing mainly calcium (such as calcium carbonate or shaved cuttle bone).

Green iguanas needing the most calcium are rapidly growing juveniles and egg-laying females. Appropriate rates of supplementation vary with the iguana's age and size, housing (inside or out), calorie intake, amount of calcium provided by the diet, and amounts of other nutrients in the diet, including phosphorus and vitamin D_3.

Attention is often given to the ratio of calcium to phosphorus in the diet. It should be in the range of 1:1 to 2:1 calcium to phosphorus (Ca:P). However, the *amounts* of dietary calcium and phosphorus are more important than the ratio. For example, if a diet contains only 0.6 percent calcium and 0.3 percent phosphorus, the Ca:P ratio is 2:1 but the amounts are deficient and a young iguana fed these intakes would develop soft bones from a life-threatening calcium deficiency. Generally, green iguanas require 1 to 1.5 percent of the diet as calcium and about 0.5 to 0.9 percent as phosphorus.

Commonly Available Calcium Supplements

	Calcium %	Phosphorus %	Calcium teaspoon (5 g)	Phosphorus teaspoon (5 g)
Calcium Carbonate	40	0	2000 mg	0 mg
Limestone	38	0	1900 mg	0 mg
Calcium Lactate	18	0	900 mg	0 mg
Calcium Gluconate	9	0	450 mg	0 mg
Bone meal	24	12	1200 mg	600 mg
Dicalcium Phosphate	24	18	1200 mg	900 mg

Supplemental Vitamin D: Green iguanas require vitamin D for a variety of functions, including the formation of strong bones by aiding the absorption of dietary calcium. Dietary vitamin D comes in two forms: vitamin D_2, which occurs in plants, and vitamin D_3, which occurs in animal tissue, especially liver. There is evidence that reptiles cannot utilize vitamin D_2, so vitamin D_3 is always recommended for green iguanas.

Basking lizards such as green iguanas can make vitamin D_3 by exposing their skin to unfiltered UV-B light rays from the sun or from special commercial lamps. Green iguanas seem to do well without dietary vitamin D_3 if they live outdoors year-round. However, a judicious amount of dietary vitamin D_3 is recommended for most green iguanas, especially those living all or part of the year indoors. As with many nutrients, vitamin D is toxic when fed in excess.

Identifying Vitamin D_3

I read the labels on the vitamin supplements in the pet store, and I couldn't find one that had vitamin D_3 in its ingredient list. Why?

Dietary vitamin D_3 may be listed on food labels as "cholecalciferol," "animal sterol," "D-activated animal sterol," "irradiated animal sterol," or as "vitamin D_3." Don't assume that the term "vitamin D" in the label ingredient list is actually D_3; it may be D_2, and unusable by your iguana.

Supplemental Protein: Studies have shown that green iguanas in the wild consume plants containing more than 27 percent protein. The author's studies have shown that green iguanas maintain normal growth, blood parameters, organ function, and health when fed more than 27 percent protein. Provide salads containing more than 20 percent protein.

As long as greens make up more than 60 percent of the diet, protein supplementation is unnecessary.

Examples of Protein Levels in Iguana Foods

(Note the inadequate protein levels in fruit)

Iguana foods	Water %	Dry matter %	Protein % fed (wet)	Protein % dry
Romaine lettuce	95	5	1.8	36
Dandelion greens	86	14	2.9	21
Zucchini squash	95	5	1.2	24
Sweet potato	73	27	6.4	24
Banana	74	26	1.0	3.8
Mango	82	18	0.5	2.8

Supplemental Fibers: Studies have shown that iguanas select high-fiber foods in the wild, and feeding trials support the view that iguanas exhibit optimal growth when fed high-fiber diets. I recommend dietary crude fiber levels of at least 20 percent.

Examples of Fiber Levels in Iguana Foods
(Note the inadequate fiber levels in fruit and some vegetables. Note also the low-water, high-fiber content of hay. A little hay in salads goes a long way.)

Iguana Foods	Water %	Dry Matter %	Fiber % fed (wet)	Fiber dry matter
Romaine lettuce	95	5	1.8	36
Dandelion greens	86	14	3.6	26
Zucchini squash	95	5	1.2	24
Carrots	88	12	3.1	17
Banana	74	26	2.4	9.2
Mango	82	18	1.8	10
Timothy hay	11	89	28	32

Green iguanas digest their food by means of hydrolytic digestion in the small intestine and fermentative digestion in the large intestine. Proteins, fats, vitamins, minerals, and simpler carbohydrates are digested by hydrolysis. In a healthy iguana, only fibers are digested by fermentation, producing short-chain fatty acids. This fermentation by symbiotic microbes in the lower bowel produces short-chain (volatile) fatty acids such as acetate, butyrate, and propionate. These are absorbed and provide energy, about two calories per gram. Moreover, they nourish the intestinal cells in the lower bowel. Optimal fiber intake leads to a healthy bowel and reduced digestive upsets, and it maintains intestinal motility and formed feces.

In the wild, iguanas take in a variety of fibers from the foods they eat. When feeding your iguana, try to match this variety through a blend of fibers from forages (grass hays such as timothy, orchard grass, meadow grasses), greens (romaine, collards, dandelion), vegetables (carrot, sweet potato), fruits (mango, papaya), and blossoms (hibiscus, dandelion).

Supplemental Vitamins: Iguanas require a full complement of water-soluble and fat-soluble vitamins. B vitamins support the nervous system, and folate (folic acid) is likely needed for successful reproduction. Vitamin C supports immune function, cartilage growth, and iron metabolism. Bioflavonoids perform as vitamin C enhancers, ensuring optimal immune function. Vitamin A is produced from dietary carotene, and functions in growth, bone structure, vision, taste, immunity, and reproduction. Vitamins E and C serve as antioxidants. Vitamin D_3 is needed for strong bone, and vitamin K functions in blood clotting.

Many vitamins are present in adequate amounts in foods eaten naturally by green iguanas. Moreover, several of the B vitamins and vitamin K are made by microbes in the healthy iguana's digestive tract and then absorbed and used by the lizard.

Once again, all iguanas need either a dietary source of vitamin D_3 or consistent exposure to unfiltered sunlight. Other essential vitamins include A and E, which should be provided in the diet. Additional vitamins may be needed when an iguana is stressed, sick, growing very rapidly, or producing eggs.

Heat from the pelleting process destroys certain vitamins. Storage of feed prior to distribution and time spent on pet-store shelves also lead to vitamin destruction. Because vitamin levels don't have to be listed on container labels of iguana pellets, it is impossible to know from the label if a commercial diet contains sufficient vitamins.

Moderate supplementation with vitamins causes no harm and helps supply nutrients in short supply. Excessive supplementation, however, risks harm to your iguana. Use supplements carefully

Supplemental Minerals: Calcium should be added with the goal being to produce a metabolic balance (homeostasis) with essential vitamins and minerals. Calcium has the narrowest range of safe intake of any nutrient. Too little calcium risks soft bones (metabolic bone disease), neurologic damage, decreased uterine motility, dystocia, and soft eggshells. Too much calcium risks secondary deficiencies of zinc, copper, and iodine, malabsorption of essential fatty acids, and formation of calcium-containing bladder stones. Too much calcium given with too much vitamin D_3 leads to life-threatening calcification (hardening) of internal organs.

Building Salads

Salads for green iguanas can be simple or complex. The simplest salad is a nutritious, palatable green (such as romaine lettuce) with a light sprinkling of calcium carbonate and a pinch of a vitamin-mineral supplement. This can be offered in the morning, followed by a late afternoon snack of one sliced strawberry. A better-balanced salad includes chopped timothy hay added at a rate of about 1 to 2 teaspoons per cupful of salad. Afternoon snacks can be alternated between fruits and vegetables, about .25 teaspoonful for a baby iguana and 1 to 2 tablespoons for a large male.

More complex salads can be fed, with some of the romaine exchanged for collard greens, beet greens, kale, spinach, and other greens. The greenery should total 70 percent of the diet. Supplements of calcium, vitamin-minerals, and hay can be added as above. The remainder (about 25 percent) can comprise an assortment of blossoms, fruits, and vegetables. For complex salads, chopped hay is essential, not optional, as with the all-romaine salad.

Water

Green iguanas are water-loving lizards. Offer clean water in bowls for drinking. Iguanas also appreciate deeper water for soaking and swimming, as well as daily mistings. You can use plastic pans (cat litter boxes, sweater boxes) in each iguana's habitat for soaking. Iguanas will soil their water, so cleanliness and good hygiene is essential. The water should be changed at least once daily and when soiled.

Baby iguanas will drink from droplets that have been sprayed onto habitat sides and cage furnishings before they learn to drink from saucers. Iguanas of all ages appreciate a fine, warm mist.

Water is also obtained from fresh salads, which contain about 85 percent water. Pellets contain only 10 to 12 percent water, so care must be taken to ensure that iguanas fed only pellets receive enough water each day. Lack of water leads to dehydration and electrolyte disturbances, which seriously impact many organ systems and can kill an iguana.

How Much is Enough? For our iguanas, we utilize three guidelines for assessment of water intake. Generally, iguanas need about .5 to 1 fluid ounce per 2.2 pounds of body weight. For the calculation, we weigh the iguana, and measure water offered and water remaining after 24 hours (accounting for evaporation in the warm habitat). Close observation of your animal is also effective. Get to know how your iguana looks when it is healthy, well fed, and well watered. Observe it closely at least twice daily. A dehydrated iguana may have any of a number of signs: sunken eyes, wrinkly dry skin, lack of fullness in the lower abdominal space, and loss of alertness or consciousness.

Additives: In-home water softeners replace calcium occurring naturally in water with sodium. Health effects from high-sodium water haven't been noticed in green iguanas, although there may be excessive salt excretion from their nasal salt glands. Excessive fluoride in water can lead to calcium deficiency, especially in reptiles fed diets with marginal calcium intakes. High fluoride occurs naturally in parts of the United States (such as the desert southwest). Baby iguanas with *fluorosis* appear to have metabolic bone disease. If your water contains too much fluoride for humans to drink safely, offer other water to your iguana.

High-Quality Food and Water

All foods offered to green iguanas should be wholesome and either fresh or carefully preserved. Salad ingredients should be washed prior to feeding and checked carefully for hazardous materials, such as twist ties, bits of plastic, and rubber bands. These items can lead to life-threatening digestive problems. Also remove sticky labels from the surfaces of fruit. Frozen vegetables marketed for human consumption are well preserved with little loss of vitamins and other nutrients. These can be offered to your iguana but thaw before offering. Avoid frozen vegetables coated with sauces and flavorings.

Produce intended for human consumption contains lower concentrations of herbicides and pesticides than those parts of produce intended to be uneaten and discarded. Take special caution if feeding produce considered inedible by humans, such as rinds from melon and peels from kiwi fruit.

The nutritional value of pellets and hay products deteriorates relatively rapidly from exposure to light, air, or heat. For example, levels of beta-carotene, a precursor of vitamin A, fall to less than 50 percent by six months after harvest, yet most commercial pellets and hay products don't reach store shelves until at least several months after hay harvest.

Supplements have limited shelf lives. Many vitamins decompose from exposure to light, air, and heat. Others are oxidized by contact with trace minerals. Select products with expiration dates and replace supplements at least every four months.

Water should be clean and free of harmful contaminants. Generally, water that is safe for you to drink is also safe for your iguanas. Most problems with water quality arise from an iguana fouling its water with either feces or decomposing food. Be sure to clean the water container daily, and offer clean water daily or as needed.

When to Feed

Green iguanas are active in the daytime and sleep at night.

Offer your iguana the bulk of its food in the morning. This is especially important if you are away in the daytime and return home late, when the iguana will be sleepy and less interested in eating. If a second meal is fed, time it to occur at least an hour or two prior to lights being turned off.

Example of a daily feeding and watering schedule:

6:30 AM: Mist with warm water.

7 AM: Lights on, prepare salad.

8 AM: Clean habitat. Clean and fill water containers. Offer salad in clean container.

5 PM: Mist with warm water. Offer clean water if needed. Offer a snack to older iguanas, or a second meal of salad to young iguanas.

8:30 PM: Remove food and water containers. Lights out.

Feeding Guidelines

How Often to Feed and Water

All iguanas should have clean water available at all times. It's best to feed all iguanas daily. Babies can be fed once or twice daily, or even more frequently if you are attempting to accustom your young lizard to a human presence. As green iguanas mature, feeding frequency can decline gradually until they are fed once daily. Although iguanas may appear fine when fed every second day, daily feeding better suits the physiology of vegetarians.

How Much to Feed

As a general rule, green iguanas may be fed as much nutritionally balanced salad as they can eat during daylight hours. Obesity won't occur in iguanas fed high fiber diets. Remove salads and fresh treats at the end of the day to avoid decomposition overnight.

Baby Green Iguanas

Newly hatched green iguanas may take a day or two to begin eating. During this time, the baby is receiving needed nutrition from its own reserves, mostly through its reabsorbed yolk sac. Most baby green iguanas in pet shops are about four weeks old. These can be started on salads of finely chopped pieces (no larger than the size of the hatchling's head). Try the softer greens, such as romaine lettuce, for small babies. House youngsters in an enclosure that is small enough for them to readily find food and water. Observe your baby iguana to ensure that it is eating. The baby should a have a full paunch, bright green skin, and an alert demeanor.

Provide drinking water in shallow saucers; we use plastic plant saucers. Very young hatchlings are often thirsty but can have trouble finding water in a large enclosure. A light misting of the walls and enclosure furnishings, or dripping water into a saucer, can help baby iguanas begin drinking. The extra humidity from misting also helps to create an appropriately humid environment.

Introduce new foods at this stage, when the young lizards are inquisitive. Offer finely chopped greens and commercial foods crumbled into bite-size pieces. Green iguanas are naturally wary of new food and require about four weeks to change diets. As the days pass, the green iguanas will nibble on the new ingredients in their salads and begin to include them as part of the daily intake.

Do not offer snacks or treats to very young iguanas. These lizards are growing very rapidly and need to fill up on highly nutritious supplemented salads to achieve their genetic potential for size, conformation, and performance.

Common feeding problems at this stage include starvation and malnutrition. Starvation is characterized by poor growth, loss of weight, and often death. It is due to poor food intake arising from a variety of causes. Temperatures may be too cool or lighting too dim, inhibiting the feeding response. It may also be due to inappropriate or unpalatable foods being offered.

Malnutrition occurs from feeding imbalanced diets, such as unsupplemented salads. Calcium deficiency is common, arising from deficiencies of dietary calcium and/or dietary vitamin D_3, or lack of UV-B. Provide your baby iguana with the extra nutrition it needs.

Juveniles and Adults

Chop all components of the salad into bite-size pieces suited to the size of your iguana. The salad can be simple or complex. Romaine has been fed successfully to green iguanas through all life stages. Other greens can be mixed in too, including dandelion, mustard, collard, kale, leaf lettuces, and bagged mixes of salad greens. Supplement to provide missing essential nutrients, especially calcium, but also trace minerals, vitamins, and fiber.

Higher calcium foods include dandelion greens, mustard greens, spinach, kale, and romaine. Alfalfa and clover hays are excellent sources of calcium, but alfalfa sprouts do not contain much calcium. Other poor sources of calcium include figs, peas, melons, mango, apple, papaya, and banana. As a general rule, higher calcium foods cannot be fed in great enough quantities to make up for the deficiencies of other calcium-deficient foods in an iguana's diet, so supplementation with calcium is recommended, as outlined above.

Commercial diets may also be offered. Crumble or moisten pellets if they are too large. Moistened foods need to be changed daily in order to avoid mold and decomposition.

Nutrition disorders are not as common in older iguanas as in hatchlings. The prevalence of calcium deficiency decreases with increasing age, but may be seen at any life stage. Another nutritional disorder is starvation, caused by offering too little food or an overly cold environment. Parasitic and infectious diseases may result from failure to keep food and water scrupulously clean. A part of feeding management is maintenance of hygienic conditions.

Intestinal upsets may arise from overfeeding snacks and treats. Excessive intake of just one food, such as apples or berries, can also lead to diarrhea. Usually digestive upsets are self-contained and resolve within a day. Owners may be alarmed by a change in the color of their iguana's stool, but often this just reflects the passage of pigments from vegetables or dyes from commercial pellets.

Breeding females may consume less food in late pregnancy because eggs fill much of their abdominal space.

During this time, offer the female the foods she especially enjoys eating, with attention given to the digestibility and nutritional balance of those foods. Despite the best of care, females often mobilize their own body stores in late pregnancy. After egg-laying, these body stores need to be replenished, so offer a nutritious diet daily.

Older Green Iguanas

Until data from feeding trials on aged green iguanas become available, my recommendations are based on the science of geriatric nutrition and personal experiences with older iguanas.

Senior iguanas tend to be less active, so they need fewer calories. However, their needs for essential nutrients remain at or near levels of younger, non-breeding iguanas. The goal is to offer fewer calories but to maintain a high-quality diet. This is accomplished most easily by offering daily salads with extra fiber. A sprinkling of extra oat tops or grass hay reduces calorie concentration while maintaining intestinal health.

Commercial Diets

A number of commercial diets are marketed specifically for green iguanas. These are comprised of plant-based ingredients usually in the form of extruded (and occasionally compressed) pellets. Most contain dyes to enhance colors, and many have sprayed-on odors to enhance acceptance (by owners as much as iguanas).

Several characteristics are common to all pellets, regardless of the formulation or quality control in manufacture. All pellets contain minimal water, so you must pay more attention to providing clean, high-quality water. If your green iguana cannot compensate for a reduced water intake, it will be predisposed to kidney disease from chronic dehydration.

Most pellets utilize the ingredients and production techniques of commercial livestock and pet food industries. While these features aren't inherently bad for lizards, they limit the scope and breadth of feeding. The ingredients in pellets are relatively few (corn, soy, poultry meal, tallow, alfalfa, and wheat), whereas the palates of green iguanas range through tropical fruits and blossoms, leaves, shoots, and sprouts. The deficiencies in ingredient variety in pellets is compensated for by differing shapes and dyes, which may please the eye of the owner more than the palate of green iguanas.

All pellets are relatively low fat; 10 or 12 percent is the limit for commercial pellets sold in paper and cardboard containers. Salads contain even less fat. The sudden introduction of high-fat foods will cause digestive upset in your iguana, leading to diarrhea and perhaps serious illness. Don't feed dog food, cat food, turtle food, parrot pellets, meats, gravies, or granola to your iguana.

Diet Assessment

Owners can assess the adequacy of their iguana's diet by careful observation. A well-fed iguana appears plump and well muscled and has a paunch to its belly. Pelvic bones should be barely visible in older juveniles and young adults, but the very young, very old, and heavily breeding females may exhibit pelvic bones with only a modest covering of subcutaneous fat. Tails should be wide at the base and well fleshed.

A well-fed iguana is alert and aware of activity in its surroundings. It should actively move about its enclosure, choosing at various times to bask, eat, dig, climb, and soak in its water dish. The iguana should eagerly eat its salads, and enjoy heavy mistings. Stools should be formed rather than sloppy, and relatively odor free.

What Not to Feed

Avoid all high-fat foods, including non-iguana pet foods, potato chips, and desserts. Also avoid foods containing theobromine (tea and chocolate), alcohol (certain candies, drinks, vanilla, and other flavorings), and caffeine (tea, coffee, and soft drinks).

Avoid avocado and plants known to be toxic to mammals, such as bracken fern, *Equisetum*, buttercup, poppy, and rhododendron. Avoid most houseplants, but pothos and nasturtium are safe. Ask your veterinarian before introducing an unknown plant to your iguana's diet.

Other foods are not toxic, but may lead to digestive or metabolic upsets in green iguanas because of high sugar content or the presence of artificial sweeteners. Avoid feeding candies, soft drinks, and sports drinks to your iguana, unless instructed to do so by your veterinarian.

Secondary Plant Compounds

Plants play a major role in the nutrition of green iguanas. Plants, however, contain much more than just nutrients. A broad category of substances, termed secondary plant compounds, impact the feeding of iguanas.

Oxalates bind calcium and trace minerals in the digestive tract, preventing their absorption and causing deficiency. Oxalates are found in varying amounts in spinach, rhubarb, cabbage, peas, potatoes, beet greens, and many other plants. These foods do *not* have to be avoided entirely, because nutritional deficiencies are risked only when these foods are fed frequently or as the sole source of nutrition without supplementation. Provision of the usual supplements of calcium and trace minerals and offering a varied diet eliminates most risk.

Goitrogens bind the trace mineral iodine, risking goiter or hypothyroidism. Goitrogens are found in highest quantities in cabbage, kale, mustard, turnip, rutabaga, and other cruciferous plants. These foods can be fed as part of a varied diet, along with a supplement that contains iodine (which can be as simple as iodized table salt). Many commercial multivitamin-mineral supplements contain adequate levels of iodine. The mineral iodine is itself toxic in large quantities (also acting as a goitrogen), so care should be taken not to overdose with commercial supplements, iodized salt, or kelp.

There are many other secondary plant compounds, and it is unfortunate that oxalates and goitrogens receive more attention than needed, while other substances are ignored. For example, many plants contain substances with hormone like activity (such as phytoestrogens in soybeans), which may impact iguanas' growth, conformation, reproduction, and health. A large number of different plant fibers may affect green iguana digestion and intestinal health. Other compounds in plants influence cognitive function, acting as stimulants or sedatives. A general rule for feeding plants to green iguanas is to offer a variety of produce from local markets of the kind and quality that you would like to eat.

Other Factors Affecting Nutrition

The very best iguana diets won't work if your iguana is kept too cold. Iguanas need heat and bright lights to maintain healthy appetites. Moreover, green iguanas kept in habitats that are too dry or offered limited water also refuse food. Even if consumed, food won't be digested or absorbed properly if an iguana is too cold or too dry.

Many of the suggestions here are guidelines, and many factors affect the diet and feeding management of iguanas in specific situations. For example, those housed outside year-round with exposure to natural sunlight don't need UVB-generating bulbs and may not need a dietary source of vitamin D_3. They also may consume trace minerals from the soil and an array of secondary plant compounds in wild plants. These iguanas will have nutritional needs that differ from those housed indoors full-time.

Feeding regimens may need to be adjusted, depending on your iguana's condition, its environment, and your management. A change of enclosure or adding cage mates, for example, can alter feeding responses, as can sexual maturity.

Females that are producing eggs have greater nutritional demands. Breeding females are subjected to an obvious stress, and stress itself increases nutrient demands, even in the absence of reproduction. Illness affects nutrition, too. Green iguanas that are sick or in pain often don't want to eat, which can impair recovery from illness and surgery. Disease itself impacts nutritional needs, and iguanas may lose weight when sick, even though food intake has been maintained.

There is no one right way to feed all green iguanas.

However, careful application of what you've read here and observation of your iguana and husbandry will result in a well-fed green iguana.

Green Iguanas as Carnivores

Nutritionists define species that naturally eat plant matter as herbivores—these include cows, horses, and rabbits. Their diets are high in fibers and other carbohydrates and, depending on the species, may be high or low in plant proteins. Dietary fat is always low, less than about 8 percent.

A green iguana is hand-fed a king mealworm.

Green iguanas are classified as herbivores, but there are times in their lives when their calories come from fat and animal-based protein instead of carbohydrates and plant-based protein.

Babies: When baby iguanas are not yet hatched and still in their eggs, they are "feeding" on the egg yolk within, receiving fat and animal protein. After hatching, the transition in digestion from carnivore to herbivore takes about four weeks. During this time, wild baby iguanas may eat food comprised of animal protein and fat with little dietary fiber—feces of adult iguanas, slugs, and small worms, for example. Such carnivory causes no harm.

Underfeeding: Green iguanas that are neglected, or otherwise fed too little food, fail to receive enough energy to meet their needs. Body tissues are mobilized to meet energy needs and the iguana's fat and muscle are used as calorie sources. At this time, the iguana is in effect "feeding" on fat and animal-based protein. The iguana appears thin, with a loss of muscling in thighs and tail as it consumes itself. This form of carnivory keeps an iguana alive until vegetarian food can be found.

Illness: A green iguana that is too sick to eat experiences metabolic changes similar to an underfed iguana. The iguana's own fat and muscle serves as energy sources. The iguana's metabolism shifts to accommodate the high-fat, high animal-based protein, low-fiber "diet." This carnivory helps to support antibody production, wound healing, and recovery from disease. The changes should be taken into account when designing diets for sick iguanas and planning transitions back to its typical high-fiber, plant-based diet during recovery.

Rebels: Every once in a while, a green iguana comes along that seems to relish small wigglies. One of my clients has a green iguana that readily eats earthworms. Other green iguanas readily eat mealworms, crickets, or pinkie mice. In long-term feeding trials with dozens of green iguanas, I've found this predilection for animal-based diets afflicts only a tiny percentage of green iguanas. There's no reason to feed wigglies to your iguana, and a diet comprising more animal- than plant-based food leads to digestive upsets. That said, a few mealworms on a weekly basis do not impact overall dietary amino acid intakes, nitrogen excretion, or kidney function.

Cousins: Although the green iguana is designed for vegetarian diets, most of its relatives are designed to eat a mix of animals and plants. These include ground iguanas (*Cyclura* sp.) and spiny-tailed iguanas (*Ctenosaura* sp.). These lizards are called omnivores because they eat plants plus invertebrates. Other cousins sport the "iguana" moniker but are entirely carnivorous. An example is the helmeted iguana, *Corytophanes cristatus*.

CHAPTER 11

DISEASES AND DISORDERS

By Roger Klingenberg, D.V.M.

The green iguana is far and away the pet reptile most commonly seen by reptile veterinarians. They easily outnumber other commonly presented reptiles, such as box turtles, bearded dragons, geckos, chameleons, and snakes. As a result of their popularity and the dedication of their owners, veterinarians now know more about their husbandry, anatomy, physiology, and medical/surgical care than of most other reptiles. This means there is a more uniform standard of veterinary care for pet iguanas.

It would take an entire book to do justice to the plethora of green iguana health problems. To highlight them, I will break the disorders into the following groups (in order of occurrence from most common to least common): nutritional/metabolic, infectious, reproductive, environmental, trauma, and parasitic.

Nutritional/Metabolic Disorders

Metabolic Bone Disease (MBD)
MBD is the most common term used to describe a complex group of bone conditions primarily seen in lizards. Other terms include rubber jaw, fibrous osteodystrophy, osteomalacia, rickets, and nutritional secondary hyperparathyroidism (NSHP). While conditions such as kidney disease and parathyroid tumors can cause these disorders, they are usually related to the disruption of the calcium uptake and

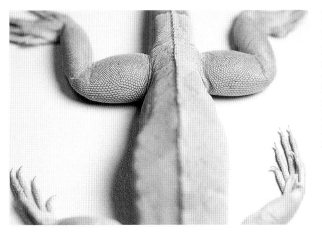

This iguana has MBD. The rear legs are so swollen and painful that the iguanas is unable or unwilling to lift its torso off the surface.

utilization in the body, resulting in bone disease.

Calcium is a vital nutrient and one of the main components of bone. Calcium is also important for muscle contractions, nerve impulses, metabolic enzyme reactions, and blood clotting. The body must maintain a certain level of calcium in the bloodstream for these functions to occur. If the body detects a low level of calcium, then the parathyroid gland (a small gland in the neck) is stimulated to release parathyroid (PTH) hormone. PTH stimulates special cells (osteoclasts) in the bone to "chew-up" the bone and make additional calcium available to the body. Once the blood level is corrected, the parathyroid gland is turned off and the osteoclasts stop breaking down bone. MBD is the result of the body lacking sufficient calcium to carry out its functions and the resulting destruction of bone in an attempt to correct this deficiency.

The most common cause of calcium deficiency is the simple lack of calcium in the diet. Another potential cause of low calcium levels is a lack of active vitamin D. Under normal circumstances, the ultraviolet (UV) exposure from basking in natural sunlight stimulates the conversion of a cholesterol metabolite in the skin into inactive vitamin D. Because most captive reptiles do not get adequate access to unfiltered sunlight, they must compensate for this through UV-producing bulbs or by taking in vitamin D_3 orally.

MBD is often noted as swollen, painful limbs. As the

condition progresses, the bones of the jaw may become weak and misshapen; this is referred to as "rubber jaw." Often, the affected reptile can't eat efficiently due to the lack of a functional jaw and pain. Fractures commonly occur as the bones become weaker and more brittle. An especially common site for fractures is in the lower back, which leads to paralysis. Muscles are also affected, which is seen as involuntary twitching of extremities and constipation due to a lack of peristalsis by the smooth muscle of the intestinal tract. If the twitching becomes more pronounced it is referred to as "tetany." Once tetany is seen, the animal is in critical condition.

Younger reptiles tend to have more subtle signs of MBD. A very common presentation for young cases is a bloated, constipated reptile with softer bones than usual. Reproducing or gravid females are more subject to MBD-problems as they have very high calcium requirements to form eggs. One of the main reasons for these females becoming egg-bound is that the lowered calcium levels cause diminished muscle activity of the uterus.

Treatment of MBD

Once recognized and understood, how do we treat this disorder?

Evaluation and Correction of Diet: In very early cases, simple dietary changes are all that is necessary to ensure that adequate calcium is available. See **Diet and Feeding Management** for information on providing a healthy, calcium-rich diet for your pet.

Vitamin D: Exposure to unfiltered UV light is the best way for inactive cholesterol precursors to change to active vitamin D in the skin. See **Heating and Humidity** for information on providing UV light to your reptile.

Hospitalization: In cases where calcium degradation has progressed, your veterinarian will probably suggest hospitalization. During hospitalization, supportive care measures such as proper heat, fluids for dehydration, enemas for constipation, and force-feeding weak iguanas are implemented. Your vet will provide oral calcium supplementation. In severe cases, they may begin injections of calcium. While hospitalized, your veterinarian will investigate secondary reasons for poor calcium utilization. Parasitism and bacterial infections of the gastrointestinal tract need to be eliminated. In addition, fractures secondary to low calcium levels are diagnosed and treated as needed.

A more recent advent in the treatment of MBD is the use of a hormone called calcitonin. In selected cases, this hormone is injected once adequate calcium levels are stabilized in the body. This drug should be used only under the supervision of a veterinarian.

Once stable, your pet will be sent home with specific instructions on how it should be fed (or force fed) and medicated, and how to provide an appropriate environment for its recovery. Hospitalization is only the first step in a long, slow rehabilitation.

Visceral Gout

All animals break down the protein they ingest in their diets into a product that can move through the blood stream and eventually be filtered out through the kidneys. Reptiles are urecotelic, which means that they form uric acid, which is poorly water-soluble. This decreased solubility is a severe liability if the kidneys are impaired or injured, or excessive uric acid is present. In either of these scenarios, the uric acid levels increase in the bloodstream to a point where they precipitate out into tissues. This deposit of urates into tissues is referred to as visceral gout.

Primary visceral gout occurs when this deposition of uric acid is due to the reptile ingesting excessive levels of protein, which, when broken down into nitrogen by-products and eventually into uric acid, exceeds the body's capacity to eliminate uric acid. Primary visceral gout can occur in iguanas fed diets that are too rich in protein. It is a common cause of death in older green iguanas fed a high meat or canned dog or cat food diet.

Secondary visceral gout occurs when even normal levels of uric acid cannot be eliminated from the body due to kidney impairment or dysfunction. Secondary visceral gout occurs primarily through chronic dehydration due to a relative lack of water. This doesn't just mean drinking water. Some reptile health experts speculate that iguanas raised in areas with low relative humidity have increased incidence of visceral gout due to chronic low-grade dehydration through evaporative water loss. Lightly misting twice daily, using live plants in enclosures, lightly spraying iguana salads, and the inclusion of a large water dish in cages can all increase the humidity without creating an overly humid, dripping environment. The misuse of aminoglycoside (Gentocin, Amikacin) and sulfonamide (Trimethoprim/sulfa) antimicrobials can also cause renal damage severe enough to cause secondary visceral gout.

Visceral gout causes such significant irritation and inflammation that affected tissues and organs are damaged. It generally has fatal consequences, even if only due to starvation from discomfort.

The bottom line is that by following a diet based primarily on plant protein and providing adequate humidity and heat, visceral gout should not occur.

Mineralization of Internal Organs

To prevent MBD, many green iguana owners supplement the diet with relatively large amounts of vitamin D_3 and calcium supplements. Once an iguana matures and growth tapers, the excess calcium and vitamin D_3 from the diet and supplements can accumulate in various internal organs. This mineralization often has fatal consequences, so take care to not oversupplement the diets of mature iguanas. Supplementation guidelines are provided in **Diet and Feeding Management**.

Renal Disease

Renal disease is becoming the most common cause of death in mature iguanas. This is probably due to a combination of a high-protein diets, oversupplementation, and chronic dehydration. However, there are no validated studies proving this.

Whether the kidneys are damaged via gout, mineralization, toxic drugs, or a combination of factors, the results are eventually the same. Once renal function has been compromised, supportive care is essential to keep the iguana feeling well enough to function. If detected early, stabilization for long periods of time, with a good quality of life, is possible in some cases. While your veterinarian can give you a fairly accurate assessment from examinations and bloodwork, the actual cause and prognosis for renal failure cannot be accurately assessed without a renal biopsy. These biopsies can be performed safely even on severely depressed patients. Only 25 percent of one kidney need be viable to perform the renal functions of the body. Once diagnosed with renal disease, your veterinarian will help decide which supportive care methods and medications are appropriate for your iguana.

Infectious Diseases

The most common infectious diseases are covered in the trouble-shooting chart, including postorbital abscesses, gum disease, oral abscesses, respiratory disease, meningitis/encephalitis, gastroenteritis, bacterial skin infections, fungal disease (blackened skin disease), and tail-based cysts. Please refer to the chart for more detail.

Frothy saliva can indicate a respiratory infection.

When treating any infectious disease you need to do whatever you can to stimulate the animal's immune system. It is generally agreed upon by reptile veterinarians that reptiles have primitive immune systems and that sick reptiles are immunocompromised. There are several factors that affect the immune status, including nutrition, hydration, age, sex, seasonal variation, and environmental factors.

Hydration

Dehydration is characterized by prominent lateral folds and a loss of skin elasticity. As this progresses, the eyes actually sink into their sockets. The easiest way to rehydrate a marginally dehydrated iguana is to place it into a shallow container of tepid water, as long as it is not in danger of drowning due to weakness. While oral consumption may help, the passive movement of water into the rectum/colon allows water to be absorbed into the body.

In situations where soaking could pose a threat to the iguana's health, fluids such as Gatorade or Pedialite can be administered through a feeding needle or catheter passed directly to the stomach. If the iguana is critically dehydrated, see a veterinarian for fluid administration by subcutaneous, intraceloemic, or intraosseous injection.

Nutritional Support

Sick iguanas are often depressed and do not want to eat, despite the fact that they are in dire need of nutrients. If the iguana is alert enough to allow force-feeding, this can be accomplished by a couple of methods. Susan Donoghue, V.M.D., author of the **Diet and Feeding Management** chapter, recommends the following force-feed mixture:

Herbivorous Diet for Force Feeding

1 6-ounce can of Ensure
1 banana
4 tablespoons of alfalfa meal

Mix and blend well. If calcium is a concern, then add 1 or 2 level teaspoons calcium carbonate to the mixture.

One advantage of this mixture is that it is quite palatable to green iguanas and often can be fed by syringe to iguanas that are able to swallow. Hold the iguana in an upright position and gently tease the mouth open with the tip of the syringe and place a couple drops of the mixture inside. Once the iguana is readily swallowing, give at a slow, steady rate. If the iguana appears to choke at any time, stop feeding and release the iguana to swallow on its own.

If your iguana cannot be force fed, ask your veterinarian about tube feeding your iguana.

Environmental Factors

Once fluid and nutritional factors are addressed, it is important to ensure the iguana has access to a usable thermal gradient. Physiologically, it is impossible for reptiles to mount a fever in response to an infective agent. However, they can behaviorally create a fever if a usable thermal gradient exists. Providing a thermal gradient is the easiest and quickest way to improve immune system integrity. Please refer to **Heating and Humidity** for specific heating recommendations.

Reproductive Disorders

Like many captive reptiles, green iguana females don't require the presence of a male to go through their reproductive cycles. It is not unusual for females that are at least two years old and weigh at least 1 pound to ovulate, often on a yearly basis.

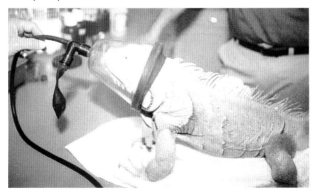

A male green iguana is anesthetized prior to surgery.

Gravid females are easily recognized by the distention of the lower abdomen. If inspected closely, the individual follicles or eggs can be seen and palpated.

With the proper hormonal stimulation, the female's ovaries, which contain dozens of BB-size follicles, begin to enlarge. The individual follicles each enlarge to the size of a grape, often in such high numbers that the iguana becomes distended in appearance. The pressure from this distention, in conjunction with the hormonal influences, causes the iguana to become agitated and often very aggressive. This aggression is probably a survival mechanism, as the heavier and slower iguana is more susceptible to its enemies. Due to the discomfort, the iguana often refuses food.

Once full follicle formation has occurred, one of two steps happens. In iguanas bred by a male, true egg formation may occur. Because it is difficult to determine when this is occurring, it is very important that a proper egg-laying substrate be provided (see **Breeding**). In the absence of such a substrate or in iguanas with low calcium levels and poor muscular contractions, the female may be unable to pass her eggs. This is referred to as egg binding, and it is imperative that a reptile veterinarian be consulted. Some iguanas can be induced to pass their eggs with calcium and hormonal injections, but surgery is often required.

If the female has never been bred, then the follicles are supposed to be reabsorbed. However, some iguanas seem to get "stuck" at the follicle stage (follicular stasis) and do not progress to form shelled eggs or reabsorb them either. These iguanas have little interest in a nesting site, usually refuse food, and are inactive and depressed. If these iguanas are not promptly taken in for surgery to remove the follicles, the follicles can rupture and cause a fatal peritonitis.

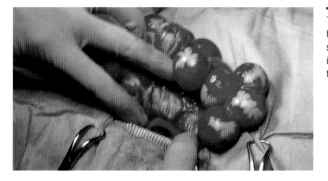

This iguana has follicular stasis, requiring a hysterectomy.

You can determine if your iguana is forming follicles or eggs through a special x-ray technique that detects the presence or absence of a shell. If true eggs are seen, set up a laying substrate. Observe the iguana carefully; if it stops eating for more than a couple days or is straining in its nest without results, consult a veterinarian. If follicles are seen, watch the iguana carefully to see if it stops eating or becomes lethargic or depressed. If any of these occur, see a veterinarian. When an iguana has follicular stasis, the treatment of choice is to spay the female. Early intervention is critical in both scenarios; it is better to err on the side of caution.

Environmental/Trauma

Injuries such as abraded nostrils, broken legs, torn nails, burns, and broken tails are addressed in the trouble-shooting chart. If your iguana is given free run of the home, it must be monitored for potential environmental hazards

This young iguana suffered a thermal burn on a hot rock, necessitating the removal of the damaged tissues from the surface of the lesion.

and for the ingestion of foreign items. I've removed wet wipes, tissues, strings, rocks, small rubber toys, and even a ballet tutu from the stomachs of impacted iguanas.

Poisonous plants and family pets are additional hazards to free-roaming iguanas. Cat bites cause very serious puncture wounds and require immediate and aggressive veterinary attention if they occur anywhere on the main body. One client reported that her green iguana was ingested by her common boa constrictor. While not usually a boa food source, boas and other snakes have been known to eat lizards.

If your iguana is allowed such freedom, "iguana proof" the living area much as you would baby or puppy proof an area. Use common sense when mixing and matching pets. In the wild, green iguanas may congregate in similar areas for protection, food sources, and occasional breeding, but they should be considered solitary animals by preference and behavior.

Parasitism

Internal Parasites

It is important for iguana owners to have fecal examinations performed on their captive pets. Intestinal parasites can interfere with food processing and absorption, cause discomfort, and damage the gastrointestinal tract.

Treat nematode parasites such as ascarids (roundworms), pinworms, and hookworms, with fenbendazole (Panacur) at 25 to 50 milligrams per kilogram, orally, once a week for at least three weeks. Treat cestodes (tapeworms) with praziquantel (Droncit) at 5 to 8 milligrams per kilogram, orally or by injection, and then repeat in two weeks. Treat protozoan agents (trichomonads and giardia) with metronidazole (Flagyl) at doses of 20 milligrams per kilogram, orally, once daily for one to five days. Treat coccidial agents with sulfadimethoxine (Albon) at a dose of 50 milligrams per kilogram, orally, once daily for three days and then every other day as needed. See your veterinarian for guidance in administering medications.

This adult imported green iguana hosts a number of ticks.

External Parasites

Firmly grasp ticks and pull (don't jerk) until they release. It is unusual to leave the head of a tick in place, as the tick damages the tissues it is attached to so they release as the tick is pulled out. Treat the wound with a topical antibiotic ointment such as Neosporin or Polysporin, if needed. In cases where a wound will not heal, systemic antibiotics may be required.

Mites can cause an iguana to become quite agitated and uncomfortable. If you observe your iguana soaking excessively, examine the iguana and its water dish for mites. If untreated, mites will cause a severe dermatitis characterized by frequent and excessive shedding in which layers of shed skin accumulate. The accumulated layers of skin can interfere with circulation and lead to the loss of toes and extremities. The adhered skin can also result in the damage of underlying scales and permanent scarring.

To treat mites, thoroughly clean the cage and use an ivermectin-based spray (5 milligrams per quart). Spray the cage and iguana lightly but thoroughly. Remove the water and food dishes from the cage until it is dry. Repeat this every four or five days for three weeks. Alternatively, use an insect strip (No Pest). In enclosures less than 50 gallons, place a .5-inch by 2-inch piece of the strip in a small jar with holes in the lid. Place the jar in the enclosure for three hours, three times a week, for up to three weeks.

A rectal prolapse is a medical emergency. See your veterinarian immediately.

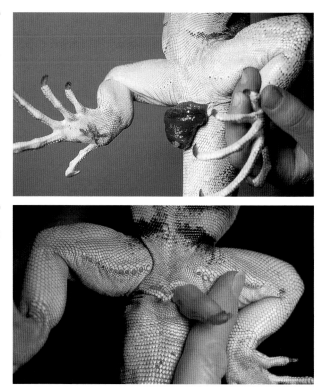

Although this appears to be a prolapsed hemipene it is really just a waxy cast built up around the hemipenes. If not easily removed, see your veterinarian.

Toxicity in reptiles with No Pest strips has been documented only in cases where excessive time of exposure, direct contact with the strip, or impaired ventilation was involved. Be sure to provide plenty of ventilation.

Green Iguana Trouble-Shooting Chart

Anatomical Region	Symptoms	Common Cause	Treatment
Eyes	Painful and swollen; the eyes and surrounding tissues bulge.	Postorbital abscess	The abscess must be lanced behind the eye and the pus evacuated, then flushed with a dilute antibiotic solution for a few days to prevent recurrence. Systemic antibiotics are recommended. Examine mouth for source (tooth abscess).
	The eye is bulging, but not surrounding tissues; the eye may be cloudy or discolored.	Infected eye; glaucoma; trauma	See a veterinarian as this requires a professional diagnosis and topical or systemic treatment.

Green Iguana Trouble-Shooting Chart

Anatomical Region	Symptoms	Common Cause	Treatment
Mouth	The jaw is soft and rubbery with distortion of the mouth.	Metabolic Bone Disease (MBD)	See section on MBD.
	The lips and mouth are swollen causing distortion, pain, and reluctance to eat.	Abscesses, especially with infected teeth	Abscesses must be lanced to evacuate pus, then flushed daily for several days. May also require systemic antibiotics and removal of infected teeth.
	The gums are swollen or red with soreness and bleeding in mouth.	Gingivitis	Commonly requires an antibiotic.
	There is crusted, dried material adhered to the lips.	Dried secretions secondary to exposure of the gums. Distortion of the gums from gum disease, MBD, or abscesses can cause secretions to accumulate and dry out.	If loose, gently remove crusts. If lips or gums are irritated, clean gently with peroxide or an antibacterial solution. Apply a light layer of petroleum jelly as needed. See veterinarian to address underlying condition.
Nostrils	The nose is rubbed and raw and may be abraded and scabbed.	Rostral abrasion, also known as "nose rub"	Caused by chronic rubbing or running into the sides of the enclosure. Correct caging so that the caging is more comfortable and secure. Avoid fine-mesh screen and cover glass so iguana is less exposed. Increase cage size and exercise. Apply antibiotic ointment to sore nose or see a veterinarian in more severe cases.
Throat	The throat is distended and inflated and appears to bulge underneath.	Respiratory infection	See section on respiratory infection below.
Respiratory System Glottis/Trachea	The iguana exhibits open-mouth breathing, coughing, or wheezing. The saliva is frothy and the head is elevated.	Respiratory infection	Most respiratory infections will respond to an increase in temperature (exposure to a useable heat gradient) if caught early. If not eating or drinking and reluctant to move, assume the iguana is in respiratory distress and see a veterinarian for antibiotics, drying agents, and potential nebulization.

Green Iguana Trouble-Shooting Chart

Anatomical Region	Symptoms	Common Cause	Treatment
Neurological	There is inappropriate movement, awkward gait, and drunken behavior, and inability to eat or drink.	Meningitis, encephalitis, overheating, or head trauma	See veterinarian for diagnosis and potential system antibiotic, anti-inflammatories, or supportive care.
	The iguana has twitching limbs and paralysis.	Thiamin deficiency, hypocalcemia, trauma	See section on MBD; treat thiamin deficiencies with oral administration of vitamin B and add Brewer's yeast to the food. An injection of B-complex coupled with dietary changes can prevent a relapse.
Gastrointestinal	The abdomen is painful and iguana is reluctant to lie down or eat.	Intestinal obstruction or occasionally a bladder stone	See a veterinarian for an x-ray immediately. Both conditions necessitate exploratory surgery.
	Exhibits straining, inability to defecate, and agitated or depressed behavior.	Constipation or occasionally a bladder stone	Constipation can be secondary to MBD—see the section on MBD. For everyday constipation, allow the lizard to soak in tepid water for fifteen to thirty minutes, two or three times each day. Oral doses of feline hairball medications may also help for severe constipation.
	Stools are bloody, mucusy, off-color, or rancid.	Gastroenteritis or parasitism	Bacterial gastroenteritis secondary to poor digestion (inadequate heat), gastrointestinal irritation due to ingesting substrates, chronic poor gastrointestinal motility (hypocalcemia), and parasitism are common. Oral metronidazole dosed at 20 mg/kg for two to three days will often clear mild bacterial and protozoal cases. Most refractory cases will need a systemic antibiotic and a fecal culture to identify the culprit.
Urinary/Reproductive System	Exhibits straining, discomfort, and inability to pass urine.	Bladder stones, urinary sludge, or renal failure	Bladder stones will probably need to be surgically removed. To promote normal kidney function, postoperative fluid care is important, as are long-term increases in humidity and access to water.
	The iguana has anorexia, weight loss, and lethargy.	Renal failure	Bloodwork, x-rays, and palpation are needed to secure a diagnosis.

Green Iguana Trouble-Shooting Chart

Anatomical Region	Symptoms	Common Cause	Treatment
Urinary/Reproductive System, Cont.	The iguana is agitated, digs, and seems to be searching for something.	Gravid female	Females can ovulate and form eggs even in the absence of a male. See **Breeding** for more information.
	An obviously gravid female is very depressed, painful, and anorectic.	Egg binding or follicular dysfunction	Even with an egg-laying site, some females will become egg bound. Other females form follicles but do not form eggs or reabsorb the follicles, leading to peritonitis or death. Treatment is hysterectomy. See a veterinarian for x-rays and a full work up.
	The cloaca, rectum, or hemipenes are protruding.	Rectal prolapse or prolapsed hemipene	All prolapses should be treated as an emergency—cover the affected tissue with a moist cloth and hold the lizard so that its feet don't tear the fragile tissue. A veterinarian will medicate and replace viable tissue, but it is very important to determine the underlying cause. The hemipenes, which are not involved in the urinary system, are amputated if the tissue is not viable.
	There is a tubular structure protruding from hemipenal pouch.	Waxy cast or hemipenal plug	Secretions that form in the hemipenal pouches can solidify and start to protrude—it shouldn't be confused with a prolapsing hemipene. Plugs can be removed by grasping and pulling. If painful or difficult to remove, a veterinarian can sedate the animal. Use lubricating ointment or antibiotics as necessary.
Skin	The skin is blackened, missing scales, and has scarring.	Fungal disease	A fungal agent, dermatophycosis, has been identified as the primary etiological agent.
	There are dry, brownish raised areas, peeling, or flaking on the skin.	Bacterial skin infection	This is often mistaken for a fungal problem, but the underlying infection is most likely due to being immunocompromised. It is often complicated by too much or too little humidity, poor sanitation, or lack of UV light exposure. Mild cases can be treated with an

Green Iguana Trouble-Shooting Chart

Anatomical Region	Symptoms	Common Cause	Treatment
Skin, Cont.			antibiotic ointment used daily. Also review your husbandry practices and provide exposure to unfiltered UV light. More involved cases may need systemic antibiotics.
	There are raised lumps under the skin.	Abscesses	Many of these cutaneous abscesses result from cage mate bites that became infected. Treat as for postorbital and oral abscesses.
	The skin is darkened, peeling, or painful.	Thermal burns, mite damage	Poor husbandry practices allow the iguana to touch the heat source—use a screen barrier to prevent contact. Do not use hot rocks. Minor burns will heal but leave scars. Serious burns require veterinary attention. Mites can also cause extensive tissue damage. Severe cases require sedation and debridement, ointment, and antibiotic treatment.
Limbs	The legs appear firm, enlarged, and more muscular than usual.	Metabolic Bone Disease (MBD)	See the section on MBD.
	Iguana is dragging or tucking a limb up against the body.	Fracture or dislocation	Severe fractures may require surgical repair. Mild fractures with little discomfort respond well to splinting.
	The toes are crooked or misaligned.	Torn ligaments and tendons of toes	Iguanas have very fine tendons and ligaments that are easily torn. It is difficult to correct this damage as bandaging and splinting often causes more damage due to circulatory impairment. Generally the toes can be left alone unless they are interfering with other toes, in which case the offending toe(s) is amputated.
	The toes are brown, blackened or stiff.	Dead toes	These are best amputated to the level of healthy tissue.
	The toes are swollen or enlarged.	Abscesses or circulatory impairment	See treatment for postorbital abscesses. Circulatory impair-

Green Iguana Trouble-Shooting Chart

Anatomical Region	Symptoms	Common Cause	Treatment
Limbs, Cont.			ment following treatment may necessitate amputation. Adhered sheds or fibers encircling a toe may be cutting off circulation and must be carefully removed. Dry sheds may need repeated applications of petroleum jelly or a hand lotion to adequately soften the dry skin.
	The iguana has masses or bumps.	Abscesses, tumors, granulomas	See treatment for postorbital abscesses. Tumors may need to be surgically removed.
Tail	Tail has masses or bumps.	Cysts, occasional abscesses	The tail of the iguana has some true sebaceous glands that can become infected and enlarged. These cysts/abscesses must be lanced, evacuated, and treated. If untreated, these masses can become large enough to interfere with the circulation and nerve supply of the tail, making it necessary to amputate the tail.
	The tail is missing with a black rubbery tip.	Regenerating tail	Fractured or amputated tails can regrow but it is very slow. No medical treatment is required.
	The tip of tail is hard, brown, and has a leathery texture.	Ischemic necrosis of tail (dry gangrene)	Tip of tail has died due to circulatory impairment, often as a result of whipping. It is best to amputate the tip, moving up to viable tissue, but removing as little as possible.

CHAPTER 12
OTHER IGUANAS

I n popular terms, all members of the family Iguanidae are called iguanas. For those of you interested in owning other iguana species, the following is an outline of iguanid lizards and their availability.

Galapagos Marine Iguana
Amblyrhyncus, one species. C.I.T.E.S. Appendix I. Protected. Not available.

Galapagos Land Iguana
Conolophus, two species. C.I.T.E.S. Appendix I. Endangered. Not available.

Spiny-tailed iguanas (*Ctenosaura* sp.) can be kept like green iguanas. Juveniles have predilection for insects.

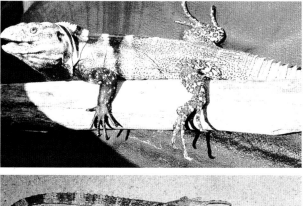

Shown is a juvenile spiny-tailed iguana *(Ctenosaura pectinata).*

Shown is a Galapagos land iguana *(Conolophus pallidus)*.

Caribbean Land and Rhinoceros Iguanas

Cyclura species. Greater Antilles and Bahamas. C.I.T.E.S. Appendix I or II. Threatened or endangered. Increasing numbers are becoming available in the hobbyist trade as a result of successful captive breeding, mostly by the private sector. Expensive and justly so.

Fiji Island Iguanas

Brachylophus, two species. Fiji and Tonga Island groups. C.I.T.E.S. Appendix I. Endangered. Not available to hobbyists but increasing success at captive breeding by a few zoos.

Spiny-Tailed Iguanas

Ctenosaura, nine species. Mexico to Panama and the Colombian Islands. Several species including some under the name *Enyaliosaurus* (not recognized as valid by many researchers). They are imported and offered in the pet trade. Captive breeding programs by hobbyists with some of the more attractive and rarer species should be implemented.

This small and pretty species, *Ctenosaura defensor*, from the Yucatan is rare in captivity.

Desert Iguanas

Dipsosaurus. Southwest United States, Mexico, islands in the Gulf of California. Most subspecies protected by state or national laws. Now rarely available in the pet or hobbyist trade. Serious efforts should be made to develop captive breeding of this species before these interesting and attractive animals become lost to hobbyists altogether.

Chuckwallas

Sauromalus, six species. Southwest United States, Mexico, islands in the Gulf of California. The entire genus is protected in most of its range by various state or national laws. Serious efforts should be made to captive breed those animals currently in captivity before they are lost to hobbyists. As a whole, they are very adaptable as juveniles but not very adaptable as wild-caught adults.

CHAPTER 13

IGUANAS OF THE WEST INDIES

By David Blair

Rhinoceros and rock iguanas of the genus *Cyclura* are medium to very large ground-dwelling lizards native to the Bahamas, Greater Antilles, and the Virgin Islands. The genus is further divided into eight species, with a total of fourteen subspecies currently recognized. Several forms are highly endangered in their natural habitat and all are listed on Appendix I of C.I.T.E.S.

The San Diego Zoo regularly breeds endangered Fiji Island iguanas *(Brachylophus fasciatus)* but they are not currently available in the herpetocultural trade.

Efforts to breed these interesting and impressive iguanas in captivity have been increasingly successful and several forms are currently available in the pet industry. The animals most likely to be offered are: the rhinoceros iguana *(Cyclura cornuta cornuta)*, native to the island of Hispaniola; the Cuban rock iguana *(C. nubila nubila)*, native to Cuba, its offshore islands and cays, and introduced in Puerto Rico; the Cayman Island rock iguana *(C. nubila caymanensis)*, from the islands of Little Cayman and Cayman Brac; and the rare and beautiful Grand Cayman blue rock iguana *(C. nubila lewisi)*, which exists in the wild only in very small numbers on Grand Cayman Island. There are also a fair number of intergrade animals, due to inadvertent mixing of the closely related *nubila* subspecies in captivity.

Care

Given the proper care, rock iguanas are very hardy in captivity and can be extremely long-lived; twenty to thirty year olds are not uncommon and some experts believe several species may live to eighty years of age.

It is easiest to begin with a hatchling or juvenile rock iguana. Older animals, if not already tame, can be difficult to work with. Although many rhinoceros iguanas eventually become quite tame, by nature they are more aggressive than Cuban and Cayman rock iguanas, which are comparatively docile in captivity.

The rhinoceros and rock iguanas are among the largest of the *Cyclura*, reaching lengths of 4 to 5 feet and weights of more than 20 pounds. Although a large adult pair eventually requires a spacious enclosure with at least 100 square feet of floor area, hatchlings may be started in smaller glass vivaria. Allow a minimum of 200 square inches for each cage mate: a 10- to 15-gallon vivarium for one and a 30- to 40-gallon for two.

Place an undertank heater beneath one end of the vivarium with a hide box over it. Use two light hoods, one with a full-spectrum bulb for daytime use and the other with a red bulb for nighttime. Control lights with auto-

Shown is a male Cuban rock iguana *(Cyclura n. nubila).* This is one of the most easily bred and readily available of the West Indies rock iguanas.

matic timers set for alternating twelve-hour periods. Temperatures should be maintained at 85-95° F during the day and 70-75° F at night. Do not use loose substrates that can accidentally be ingested. Instead, use indoor-outdoor carpet or butcher paper—both are easy to clean and replace. Always supply water to hatchlings in a small, shallow bowl so that they do not become dehydrated.

Food

Rock iguanas, like their relative the green iguana, are chiefly vegetarian. The following mix may be fed to adults two to four times a week:

The Grand Cayman blue rock iguana *(Cyclura n. lewisi)* is an endangered species that is now bred in some numbers by private herpetoculturists. As a rule, members of this species tend to become quite tame.

* Four to five leafy, green vegetables (parsley, chard, collards, turnip greens, mustard greens, beet greens, kale, or romaine).

* Grated carrots and squash.

* Two to three fruits (apples, pears, grapes, melons, bananas, mangos, papayas, and berries).

* Dry, low-fat dog food, or monkey-chow biscuits (soaked in water first to soften) in small amounts.

* Dust mixture once or twice a week with one part vitamin/mineral supplement and one part calcium supplement.

Feed this same mixture, but more finely chopped, to young iguanas on a daily basis. Also offer crickets, waxworms, mealworms, or butterworms twice a week. You can add occasional pinkie mice to the diet.

Sexual Maturity: If properly cared for, rock iguanas grow rapidly, usually reaching 20 to 24 inches long within the first year. Cuban and Cayman iguanas can reach sexual maturity as early as their third or fourth year. Male rock iguanas grow to a much larger size than females and have much higher dorsal crest scales. Rhinoceros iguanas, on the other hand, mature somewhat later, in their fourth or fifth season. Males reach only a slightly larger size than females, although their

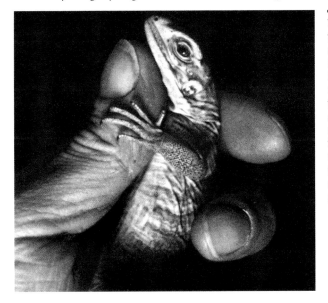

This is a captive-bred rhinoceros iguana. Increasing numbers of these animals are becoming available thanks to the concerted efforts of a few dedicated herpetoculturists.

head and jowls are proportionately larger. Both sexes have the characteristic enlarged scales or horns on the snout, which give this species its common name. The femoral pores on mature males of both species are also more highly developed, often with comblike structures extending from them, especially during the breeding season.

On rare occasions, rock iguanas have been raised to maturity and even reproduced successfully entirely indoors under artificial conditions, but there is no question that access to natural sunlight in outdoor enclosures is highly beneficial for long-term maintenance. In warmer parts of the United States, such as Southern California or Florida, animals may be kept outdoors year round, as long as shelters are provided with supplemental heat sources during winter months and when nighttime temperatures drop below 55-60° F. In other areas, they can be placed into outdoor enclosures throughout the warm summer months, the period in which most courtship and reproductive activities take place.

Most *Cyclura* iguanas breed in May and June during a brief two- to three-week mating season. Eggs are laid approximately forty days later and are among the largest produced by any lizard in the world. Provide gravid females with a sandy area outdoors or a large nesting box indoors filled with moist sand or potting soil. Remove the eggs and incubate them artificially in plastic containers half-filled with moist vermiculite. At 86° F, eggs hatch after approximately ninety days, usually between September and November. Hatchlings begin to feed after seven to ten days and should be kept warm indoors during the first winter. They may then be placed into outdoor enclosures in early summer if temperatures permit. Frequent handling of young iguanas helps keep them tame and accustoms them to interaction with their owners.

If these basic requirements are met, rhinoceros and rock iguanas make hardy and responsive captives that will thrive for many years. In fact, as many tortoise and parrot owners do for their animals, you may even need to include these long-lived iguanas in your will.

Appendix: 1

QUESTIONS AND ANSWERS

The following are answers to questions submitted after the publication of the first edition of this book.

FAQ: *I have a male iguana that I raised from a baby and it is now just over three years old. Until recently, he has been a tame and wonderful pet that I would often let free in my living room. A few weeks ago he started attacking and biting me, as well as my dog and the other iguanas I keep. What is going on? Am I going to have to get rid of him?*

From the information you provide, it appears that your male is now sexually mature and in breeding season. This happens primarily in the late winter and spring and usually phases out by summer, although some iguanas may re-enter a breeding state in the fall. Male iguanas have very large testes that produce large amounts of the male hormone testosterone during the breeding season. The result is an increase in sexual drive, as well as territorial and aggressive behavior. Such males challenge and attack intruders and may also attack, as well as continuously try to breed with, any female iguanas in close proximity.

In the relatively small enclosures where captive iguanas are usually kept, there is little outlet for the territorial, aggressive, and sexual behaviors of males. They can sometimes kill females. The behavior of males varies significantly from individual to individual.

Males should be carefully monitored when kept with females and removed when severe biting, particularly in areas other than the back of the neck, is observed. You should not keep two males together unless you can provide a very large area for the animals, with shelters and a varied landscape. In very large enclosures (room sized and larger) with a variety of landscaping that vertically stratifies space (e.g., creating walls of plants) and with large shelters (e.g., pipes), females usually have the space to escape and hide from overly aggressive males. Furthermore, a variety of behavioral displays and interactions provide an outlet for the sexual and aggressive drives of males. So keep your male in its enclosure, do not handle it, and monitor its behavior carefully if you intend to breed it. By late spring or summer, it should return to normal.

Certain males are so aggressive that the only solution is to remove them from a breeding group and keep them in isolation until the end of the breeding season.

FAQ: *I have a twelve-year-old daughter who wants a baby green iguana. What is your recommendation?*

A green iguana would not be my first choice as a pet for a twelve year old. As stated at the beginning of this book, there are several factors that do not make the green iguana an ideal pet, including adult size, the risk of salmonellosis (if proper hygiene procedures are not followed), and possible aggression when males reach sexual maturity. There are smaller species of lizards, including bearded dragons, blue-tongue skinks, and leopard geckos, that are more manageable than green iguanas. The main question should be whether you, the parent, are willing to assume the responsibility of a green iguana, including making sure it is properly caged and provided for. You will also need to implement hygiene procedures, make sure nails are kept trim, and monitor any handling of the green iguana by your child.

Selection of an iguana plays an important role in the kind of pet you will have. Pick out an animal that is relatively calm when approached. Remember, the behavior of some male iguanas can change drastically after they reach sexual maturity, so a female is a better bet for a child. Look at some adult animals before you buy so you are aware of what you're getting into. Captive-raised animals that are tame and easily handled are generally a good choice as pets because you will be able to determine their temperament at the time of purchase. Above all, be responsible and use common sense. Remember, your twelve-year-old is still a child and it is critical that you supervise any interactions with a green iguana.

FAQ: *My female green iguana is looking fat but she hasn't eaten in almost five weeks. Occasionally she feeds on insects or fuzzy mice. I love her and am afraid she's going to die.*

I suspect that your female is gravid. If you are truly concerned, take your iguana to a veterinarian to verify this condition. Gravid females typically go off feed for several weeks prior to laying. If you don't have a suitable egg-laying site, it may be retaining eggs. It is also important to provide extra calcium at this point in time. See **Breeding** for information on building a nest box.

As long as your female appears generally healthy, don't worry. If it appears unusually sluggish or is losing too much weight, take it to a veterinarian.

FAQ: *I bought a green iguana because I saw one at a herp show and was delighted by how tame it was. My iguana is now a year old and still won't let me pick it up without going crazy or lashing me with its tail. What can I do?*

I'd recommend starting from scratch. Select a hatchling or very young animal that is relatively calm when you first reach out to pick it up and calms down after you let it move from hand to hand. Only experience will teach you this, but you'll notice differences between animals. Some iguanas quickly calm down and start inspecting your hands by calmly flicking their tongue and moving from hand to hand. That's the kind of animal you want to start with if you want a pet. Your current iguana will probably remain wary and aggressive and never become a good pet. You can keep it as a display animal or try to sell it.

FAQ: *My male green iguana recently charged at me with mouth open. What should I do?*

Remember, iguana bites are serious and under no circumstance should you put yourself in a position where you may be bitten. Male green iguanas that are actively aggressive are displaying territorial behavior and challenging you. It is important that you use negative reinforcement to alter this behavior pattern. You need to show that you are the boss, that you will not be intimidated, and that this behavior will not be tolerated. This requires a certain degree of confidence and it is not without risk. If uncertain that you can deal with the situation, consult an expert, because a single bite by a large male iguana can be a serious affair. See **Iguanas as Pets** for information on handling an aggressive iguana.

If you are a woman, also consider the following: in a published paper three veterinarians found a correlation in the sudden aggression of once-tame male iguanas and menstruation in their female owners (Frye et al, 1991). In these cases, only the female owners were attacked. The aggressive behavior in these iguanas is believed to be a behavioral response to pheromones released by menstruating women. Options as to what to do with pet male iguanas in these situations range from keeping them in isolation during periods of menstruation, to castration, to selling or giving away the animals.

FAQ: *Are green iguanas easy lizards to keep?*

If you mean can they be raised under simple and inexpensive conditions, the answer is no. They require large enclosures, lighting, and heat. If you mean are they easy to feed and maintain, the green iguana is one of the easiest lizards to keep in captivity.

FAQ: *I own a pet store. I have followed all the instructions in your book on how to keep baby iguanas. Usually I have good luck but there are times when I get a group of iguanas, particularly baby iguanas, and they all die. What am I doing wrong?*

Possibly nothing. Welcome to the animal trade. Many factors contribute to the high death rate of imported iguanas. There are times when all the iguanas in a given group of imports are ill and you will not be able to do much to save them, particularly with babies, which are generally difficult to treat. High mortality rates in imports can be widespread at certain times of the year. Importers speak of good versus bad groups of iguanas. In bad groups, mortalities of 90 percent or more in the first two or three weeks are not uncommon. Widespread viral infections, respiratory infections, and gastroenteritis are common causes of death in these groups. Realistically, there may be nothing much you can do for these animals, although you can take several ill or dead animals to a veterinarian to have him or her determine any disease and a possible course of treatment. You have to weigh the possible costs of treatment, chances of success, and whether they are justifiable. In my experience, the prognosis for recovery is not very good with baby iguanas, but this depends on the type of disease involved. If a large number of animals and significant amounts of money are involved, then consult a veterinarian as quickly as possible. If the animals are in any way guaranteed, consider returning the animals to your supplier for a credit or a refund.

The reasons for widespread diseases in certain groups of imported iguanas are two-fold. First, iguanas are often maintained under inadequate and unsanitary conditions in their country of origin. Foul water is a primary vector for the spread of disease and overcrowding is also a factor. Another reason is the procedures involved with enforcing some of the wildlife laws. Iguanas are C.I.T.E.S. Appendix II animals, which means that permits are required for exportation and importation. Delays in the bureaucratic system can contribute to the high death rate and demise of Appendix II animals.

FAQ: *I have a pet iguana. Every once in a while, I'll notice that part of a toe swells up. Later the end dries up and falls off. My iguana is now missing three toe ends. What causes this?*

Believe it or not this is not an uncommon complaint or question among iguana owners. In my experience, the primary cause of this problem is carpet threads. Invariably, when someone brings an iguana to me with this condition, close observation will reveal carpet fibers, fine and nearly invisible, wrapped around and tightly constricting a toe, thus cutting off the blood supply. A conversation with the owner usually reveals that the iguana is allowed to run around the house at various times and that the floor is covered with carpet. If noticed early, the obvious treatment is to carefully cut off the fibers using very fine scissors. In some cases antibiotics may also have to be administered and a visit to the veterinarian is required. If the above is not the case, it may be an infection. Consult your veterinarian.

Appendix: 2

ORGANIZATIONS

International Iguana Society

The International Iguana Society is a nonprofit corporation dedicated to the preservation of the biological diversity of iguanas. As presently defined, the family Iguanidae consists of the genera *Amblyrhynchus, Brachylophus, Conolophus, Ctenosaura, Cyclura, Dipsosaurus, Iguana,* and *Sauromalus.* Many species of iguanas are in immediate danger of extinction, especially the West Indian rock iguanas of the genus *Cyclura.*

Membership dues support active conservation projects, and in addition, you will receive a subscription to the *Iguana Times*, a quarterly newsletter that contains great information on iguanas.

Direct inquiries to:

International Iguana Society
P.O. Box 36618
Bonita Springs, FL 34136
www.iguanasociety.org

Association of Reptilian and Amphibian Veterinarians (ARAV)

What is the ARAV?

The Association of Reptilian and Amphibian Veterinarians (ARAV) is a nonprofit international organization of veterinarians and herpetologists founded in 1991. ARAV's goal is to improve reptilian and amphibian husbandry and veterinary care through education, exchange of ideas, and research. The ARAV promotes conservation and humane treatment of all reptilian and amphibian habitat preservation.

Benefits of Membership

Membership is open to anyone with an interest in veterinary care of reptiles and amphibians. Membership benefits include subscription to the quarterly bulletin of the ARAV, reduced tuition for the annual conference, annual conference proceedings and membership directory, support of conservation and research funds, and pride in supporting the advancement of reptilian and amphibian medicine and surgery.

Direct inquiries to:

Association of Reptilian and Amphibian Veterinarians
P.O. Box 605
Chester Heights, PA 19017
www.arav.org
610-358-9530
Fax: 610-892-4813

Appendix: 3

HYGIENE

The following recommendations were developed by The Pet Industry Joint Advisory Council (PIJAC) in collaboration with the Centers for Disease Control and Prevention.

Reptile Handling

Reptiles carry the *Salmonella* bacterium, which can make people sick. To reduce the chance of infection, follow these simple steps for safe handling.

* Always wash your hands thoroughly after you handle your pet reptile, its food, and anything it has touched.

* Keep your pet reptile in a habitat designed for it; don't let it roam around the home.

* Keep your pet reptile and its equipment out of the kitchen or any area where food is prepared.

* Don't nuzzle or kiss your pet reptile.

* Keep reptiles out of homes where there are children under twelve years of age or people with weakened immune systems. Children under five should handle reptiles only with adult/parental guidance and should always be instructed to wash their hands afterward.

Contact PIJAC for more information:

PIJAC
1220 19th Street N.W.
Suite 400
Washington D.C. 20036
202-452-1525
Fax: 202-293-4377

FINDING A NEW HOME FOR YOUR IGUANA

Every year, thousands of iguana owners decide they can no longer keep Iggy. They don't have the space, they don't have the time, they've lost interest, or Iggy has become too nasty. If you give up your pet iguana, please do so responsibly.

What Not To Do

Never release an iguana in the wild or anywhere else. It is against the law and your iguana will probably die of cold come winter. In addition, the release of green iguanas generates bad publicity that negatively impacts those who keep reptiles.

Do not call the local zoo to see if they are interested in green iguanas. In major cities, zoos get more calls about green iguanas than they can handle; they do not have the space to devote to the glut of unwanted green iguanas.

What To Do

Remember that finding a home for an unwanted green iguana is similar to finding a home for an unwanted dog or cat. Here are some basic steps:

1) You can take out an ad in the local paper and offer your green iguana and caging for a reasonable price. Remember, there is a glut of large green iguanas so do not expect to make money from the sale of your iguana.

2) Contact a pet store that carries reptiles. Some stores take a limited number of healthy pet iguanas for free and, as

a service, sell them inexpensively so they can find a home.

3) Contact a local herpetological society. Some have adoption programs and may be able to help your iguana find a home.

4) Take your green iguana to an animal control agency or animal rescue organization where it will be put up for adoption.

5) Sick or unusually aggressive green iguanas should be euthanized. The headache and cost of treatment should not be passed on to another pet owner, nor should the risks of dealing with an aggressive and potentially dangerous animal.

REFERENCES

Allen, Mary. 1992. "Nutritional Considerations in Feeding Reptiles." A presentation at the 15th International Herpetological Symposium on Captive Propagation and Husbandry, St. Louis, MO. (Paper should be available in the 1992 IHS Proceedings.)

Beltz, Ellin (ed.). 1989. "Care in Captivity," Chicago Herp Society: 42-43.

Boyer, T. 1991. "Common Problems and Treatment of Green Iguanas *(Iguana iguana)*." *Bulletin of the Association of Amphibian and Reptilian Veterinarians* 1(1):8-11.

Boyer, T. (ed.). 1991. "Green Iguana Care." *Bulletin of the Association of Amphibian and Reptilian Veterinarians* 1(1):12-14.

Burghardt, G. and S. Rand. 1982. *Iguanas of the world: Their behavior, ecology and conservation.* Noyes Publications:Park Ridge, NJ.

Cogan, R.C. 1989. "The captive husbandry and breeding of the green iguana *Iguana iguana.*" Proceedings of the 13th Herpetological Symposium on Captive Propagation and Husbandry.

Frye, F. 1991. *A Practical Guide for Feeding Captive Reptiles.* Krieger Publishing:Malabar, FL.

Frye, F. 1991. *Reptile Care: An Atlas of Diseases and Treatments.* T.F.H. Publications:Neptune, NJ.

Frye, F., Mader, D., and B. Centrofanti. 1991. "Interspecific (Lizard: Human) Sexual Aggression in Captive Iguanas *(Iguana iguana).*" *Bulletin of the Association of Amphibian and Reptilian Veterinarians* 1(1):4-6.

Mendelsohn, H. 1980. "Observations on a Captive Colony of *Iguana iguana*" in *Reproductive Biology and Diseases of Captive Reptiles.* eds. Murphy J. and J. Collins. *Society for the Study of Amphibians and Reptiles* 119-124.

Rodda, G.M. 1990. "Sex and violence in South America: Tactics of reproduction in the green iguana." *Tucson Herp. Soc. Newsl.* 3(2):15-19.

Troyer, K. 1987. "Small differences in daytime temperature affect digestion of natural food in a herbivorous lizard, *(Iguana iguana)*." *Comp. Biochem. Physiol.* 87a(3):623-626.

Troyer, K. 1984. "Diet selection and digestion in *Iguana iguana*, the importance of age and nutrient requirements." *Oecologia* (Berlin) 61:201-202.

Troyer, K. 1983. "The biology of iguanine lizards: Present status and future directions." *Herpetological* 39:317-328.

Ullrey, Duane. 1992. "Nutrition Principles and Dietary Husbandry of Reptiles and Amphibians" A presentation at the 15th International Herpetological Symposium on Captive Propagation and Husbandry, St. Louis, MO. (Paper should be available in the 1992 IHS Proceedings.)

Wright, K. 1992. "The use of anthelmintics (dewormers) in captive herbivorous reptiles." *The Vivarium* 3(6):23-25.

INDEX

ABOUT THE AUTHOR

Philippe de Vosjoli is a highly acclaimed author of the best-selling reptile-care books, The Herpetocultural Library Series. His work in the field of herpetoculture has been recognized nationally and internationally for establishing high standards for amphibian and reptile care. His books, articles, and other writings have been praised and recommended by numerous herpetological societies, veterinarians, and other experts in the field. Philippe de Vosjoli was also the cofounder and president of The American Federation of Herpetoculturists, and was given the Josef Laszlo Memorial Award in 1995 for excellence in herpetoculture and his contribution to the advancement of the field.